BLACKSTO

GENERAL POLICE DUTIES

BLACKSTONE'S POLICE

GENERAL POLICE DUTIES

First Edition

Huw Smart and
John Watson

Consultant Editor:
Fraser Sampson

UNIVERSITY PRESS

OXFORD

UNIVERSITY PRESS

Great Clarendon Street, Oxford OX2 6DP

Oxford University Press is a department of the University of Oxford.
It furthers the University's objective of excellence in research, scholarship,
and education by publishing worldwide in

Oxford NewYork

Athens Auckland Bangkok Bogotá Buenos Aires Cape Town
Chennai Dar es Salaam Delhi Florence Hong Kong Istanbul Karachi
Kolkata Kuala Lumpur Madrid Melbourne Mexico City Mumbai Nairobi
Paris São Paulo Shanghai Singapore Taipei Tokyo Toronto Warsaw

with associated companies in Berlin Ibadan

Oxford is a registered trade mark of Oxford University Press
in the UK and certain other countries

Published in the United States
by Oxford University Press Inc., New York

A Blackstone Press Book

British Library Cataloguing in Publication Data

Data available

Library of Congress Cataloging in Publication Data

Data available

ISBN 1-84174-292-9

1 3 5 7 9 10 8 6 4 2

Typeset by Style Photosetting Limited, Mayfield, East Sussex
Printed in Great Britain
on acid-free paper by
Ashford Colour Press Limited, Gosport, Hampshire

CONTENTS

INTRODUCTION

Before you get into the detail of this book, there are two myths about Multiple Choice Questions (MCQs) that we need to get out of the way right at the start:

1. that they are easy to answer
2. that they are easy to write

Take one look at a professionally designed and properly developed exam paper such as those used by the Police Promotion Examinations Board or the National Board of Medical Examiners in the US and the first myth collapses straight away. Contrary to what some people believe, MCQs are not an easy solution for examiners and not a 'multiple-guess' soft option for examinees.

That is not to say that *all* MCQs are taxing, or even testing — in the psychometric sense. If MCQs are to have any real value at all, they need to be carefully designed and follow some agreed basic rules.

And this leads us to myth number 2.

It is widely assumed by many people and educational organisations that anyone with the knowledge of a subject can write MCQs. You need only look at how few MCQ writing courses are offered by training providers in the UK to see just how far this myth is believed. Similarly, you need only to have a go at a few badly designed MCQs to realise that it *is* a myth none the less. Writing bad MCQs is easy; writing good ones is no easier than answering them!

As with many things, the design of MCQs benefits considerably from time, training and experience. Many MCQ writers fall easily and often unwittingly into the trap of making their questions too hard, too easy or too obscure, or completely different from the type of question that you will eventually encounter in your own particular exam. Others seem to use the MCQ as a way to catch people out or to show how smart they, the authors, are (or think they are).

There are several purposes for which MCQs are very useful. The first is in producing a reliable, valid and fair test of knowledge and understanding across a wide range of subject matter. Another is an aid to study, preparation and revision for such examinations and tests. The differences in objective mean that there are slight differences in the rules that the MCQ writers follow. Whereas the design of fully validated MCQs to be used in high stakes examinations which will effectively determine who passes and who fails have very strict guidelines as to construction, content and style, less stringent rules apply to MCQs that are being used for teaching and revision. For that reason, there may be types of MCQ that are appropriate in the latter setting which would not be used in the former. However, in developing the MCQs for this book, the authors have tried to follow the fundamental rules of MCQ design but they would not claim to have replicated the level of psychometric rigour that is — and has to be — adopted by the type of examining bodies referred to above.

These MCQs are designed to reinforce your knowledge and understanding, to highlight any gaps or weaknesses in that knowledge and understanding and to help focus your revision of the relevant topics.

I hope that we have achieved that aim.

Good luck!

ACKNOWLEDGEMENTS

As qualified police trainers, we have written this book to complement *Blackstone's Police Manuals* and to provide a source of improving knowledge of police-related legislation. It is important to recognise that full study of the relevant chapters in the *Police Manuals* is recommended before attempting the Questions and Answers.

Particular attention should be paid to **Answers** section and students should always ask themselves, 'Why did I get the question wrong?' and just as importantly 'Why did I get the question right'. Combining the information gained from self-questioning and the information contained in the **Answers** section should lead to a greater understanding of the subject matter.

We wish to thank Alistair MacQueen for his faith, Heather Saward for pulling it all together and Fraser Sampson for his words of wisdom. Thanks also to Jane Kavanagh at Oxford University Press for her continuing support of the project.

Huw would like to thank Julie for her patience and understanding during long evenings and weekends of work, Ian, Debbie, Theresa and Vince at Detail Technologies Limited for all their hard work.

John would like to thank Sue for her patience and understanding during long evenings and weekends of work and remind David, Catherine and Andrew that Daddy is not just the man who sits in the corner working on his computer.

1 POLICE

This first chapter deals with the highly regulated area of police conduct and performance. Much of what is contained within this area is to be found in the relevant Regulations. However, it is important to remember that these Regulations are themselves made under Acts of Parliament — primarily the Police Act 1996 and some restrictions on police officers' lives come directly from the Act itself.

Although the concept of police misconduct and poor performance may seem an unpalatable subject to start your course of study, the maintenance of proper professional standards is paramount to all police officers, supervisors and managers — and the communities they serve.

QUESTIONS

Question 1

Police authorities are under a duty to comply with 'best value' requirements.

From where does this duty come?

[A] It is a statutory duty.
[B] It is a Home Office directive.
[C] It is a Police Regulations directive.
[D] It is a directive from Her Majesty's Inspectorate of Constabularies.

Question 2

Constable TURNER was a member of a trade union prior to joining the police. She left the union as she had heard she couldn't be a member whilst a serving officer. However, she has recently heard that she can in fact be a member of a union and a serving officer.

Which of the following is correct in relation to this?

[A] She can re-join the union with the permission of her chief officer.
[B] She cannot re-join the union, police regulations prohibit it.
[C] She cannot re-join the union, statutory law prohibits it.
[D] She can re-join the union with the permission of her police authority.

Question 3

To which of the following officers do the Police (Efficiency) Regulations 1999 apply?

[A] A probationary constable.
[B] An Assistant Chief Constable/Commander.
[C] A Chief Inspector.
[D] A civilian enquiry officer.

Question 4

Special Constable SMITHERS is an officer with Northshire Constabulary. Due to serious public disorder he is sent, as part of a mutual aid scheme, to Eastland Police on a Police Support Unit (PSU) duties. Eastland Police area is *not* adjacent to Northshire Constabulary area and they are some distance apart.

Considering the actions of Northshire Police, which of the following is true?

[A]   Their action is incorrect, the special constable has no powers in Eastland.

[B]   Their action is incorrect, special constables may not be used in mutual aid.

[C]   Their action is correct, the special constable has all his powers and privileges.

[D]   Their action is correct, however the special constable cannot use his powers of arrest.

Question 5

SMITHSON has written a letter of complaint to the police regarding Constable BRANDRICK and her investigation of a burglary. The letter outlines that the officer did not make any local enquiries or call a Scenes of Crime Officer (SOCO) to examine the scene. The letter raises SMITHSON'S concerns about the officer's ability. Constable BRANDRICK has four years' police service.

How should BRANDRICK'S Sergeant deal with the letter?

[A]   It must be investigated as a complaint against police only.

[B]   It must be forwarded to the complaints department for investigation.

[C]   It must be dealt with as 'unsatisfactory performance' only.

[D]   It can be dealt with either as unsatisfactory performance or a complaint.

Question 6

Constable DOUGHTY has been served with a notice requiring him to attend a first interview in relation to unsatisfactory performance. He wishes to take someone with him to the interview to advise him.

Who can the officer take with him to the interview?

[A] Anyone who is a serving officer in any police force.
[B] Anyone who is a serving member of his own police force.
[C] Anyone at all, provided they are not a solicitor.
[D] Anyone at all, including a solicitor.

Question 7

Constable DOUGHTY is now at his first hearing and is accompanied by his friend, Constable GRIFFITHS.

Who is entitled to make representations at this hearing?

[A] Only Constable DOUGHTY may make representations.
[B] Only Constable GRIFFITHS may make representations.
[C] Both of them may make representations.
[D] Both of them must make representations.

Question 8

An officer subject to unsatisfactory performance, following formal interviews, is subject to a 'reasonable period' under which they must improve their performance.

How long is this 'reasonable period' normally?

[A] Not less than two months and no more than six months.
[B] Not less than three months and no more than six months.
[C] Not less than three months and no more than eight months.
[D] Not less than two months and no more than eight months.

Question 9

Prior to an inefficiency hearing, under the Police (Efficiency) Regulations 1999, the personnel officer must send a written notice to the member concerned outlining certain details.

How many days before the date fixed for the hearing must the notice be sent?

[A]   Twenty-one days.
[B]   Fourteen days.
[C]   Seven days.
[D]   Twenty-eight days.

Question 10

Constable EVERITT is appearing before an inefficiency hearing.

Which of the following statements is correct?

[A]   She has an absolute right to be legally represented.
[B]   She has no right to be legally represented.
[C]   She has the right to be legally represented only where the supervising officer has given written notice of that right.
[D]   She has the right to be legally represented only where the supervising officer has given verbal notice of that right.

Question 11

A police Sergeant has been using overbearing conduct (both words and behaviour) towards a Constable on his team.

What part of the new Code of Conduct has the Sergeant breached?

[A]   Fairness and impartiality.
[B]   Use of force and abuse of authority.
[C]   Politeness and tolerance.
[D]   Performance of duties.

Question 12

A fellow officer approaches you and seeks your advice regarding an officer who has been suspended from duty. The suspended officer will shortly be sitting the national promotion examination, and wonders whether he will be able to take the exam whilst still suspended.

What advice should you give him?

[A] No he cannot, not while he is still suspended.
[B] Not unless his chief officer has expressly authorised it.
[C] He can, unless his chief officer has expressly forbidden it.
[D] He can, but he must be accompanied by an officer from the Police Federation.

Question 13

Which of the following complaints against police *must* be referred to the Police Complaints Authority?

[A] Any assault, including common assaults.
[B] An assault amounting at least to actual bodily harm (s. 47 of the Offences Against the Person Act 1861).
[C] An assault amounting at least to grievous bodily harm (ss. 18 and 20 of the Offences Against the Person Act 1861).
[D] Only where the death of a person is involved is a mandatory referral needed.

Question 14

Section 65 of the Police Act 1996 defines a complaint in relation to the recording and investigation of complaints against police officers.

How, if at all, does this definition apply to special constables?

[A] It applies as they are 'a member of a police force'.
[B] It applies, but only in relation to times they are 'on duty'.
[C] It does not apply as they are not 'a member of a police force'.
[D] It does not apply as they are not 'police officers'.

Question 15

FARR is aware that special constables are entitled to free travel on the local buses. FARR makes a false warrant card with the term 'Special Constable' on it and a picture of himself. Every day he travels on the bus and produces this card to obtain free rides. He never states he is a special constable, merely shows the bus driver his card.

Has FARR committed an offence of impersonating a police officer contrary to s. 90(1) of the Police Act 1996?

[A]   No, as he did not say he was a special constable.
[B]   No, as the legislation does not apply to impersonating special constables.
[C]   Yes, provided his intention was to deceive.
[D]   Yes, provided his intention was to obtain an advantage.

Question 16

Superintendent BOLIN is a Divisional Commander, and as such has 24-hour responsibility. She is at home one evening having drunk half a bottle of wine, when an Inspector phones her seeking her attendance at a firearms incident. She refuses to go because she has been drinking the wine. Considering the Code of Conduct as it relates to sobriety, has she committed misconduct by drinking the wine?

[A]   No, she can refuse to attend at no discredit to herself.
[B]   No misconduct, however it could be unsatisfactory performance.
[C]   Yes, Home Office guidance suggests she is 'on duty'.
[D]   Yes, as she is not 'drunk' she is under an obligation to attend.

ANSWERS

Question 1

Answer **A** — The requirement comes from s. 3 of the Local Government Act 1996, which makes it a statutory duty. Police authorities are defined as best value authorities by s. 1(d) of the Act, therefore answers B, C and D are incorrect.

Question 2

Answer **C** — Section 64 of the Police Act 1996 prohibits a police officer from becoming a member of a trade union. It is a legal requirement and not a police regulations requirement and therefore answer B is incorrect. Had she not left the union, she could have sought permission from her chief officer to *remain* a member of that union. She cannot re-join, making answers A and D incorrect.

Question 3

Answer **C** — The Police (Efficiency) Regulations 1999 do not apply to officers above the rank of superintendent (therefore answer B is incorrect), probationers (therefore answer A is incorrect) nor civilian staff (therefore answer D is incorrect). All these members of staff have their own procedures, but are not covered by the above Regulations.

Question 4

Answer **C** — In general, special constables have powers and privileges in their own areas or adjoining areas only. However, they can be used in mutual aid schemes, so answer B is incorrect. Where so used, they retain their powers and privileges, which include powers of arrest, and therefore answer D is incorrect. Answer A is incorrect because Smithers is on mutual aid; were he there on holiday he would not have any powers.

Question 5

Answer **D** — Smithson, a member of the public is complaining about the performance of the officer's duty. This is part of the misconduct procedures, which the Sergeant may investigate without forwarding to complaints department and therefore answer B is incorrect. However, it is clearly evidence of unsatisfactory performance and although the procedures for performance improvement and the investigation of complaints are quite separate, there may be cases, as here, where they overlap. In deciding which course of action to take, the Sergeant can consider both procedures and is not mandated to use either one and therefore answers A and C are incorrect.

Question 6

Answer **A** — Constable Doughty is entitled to be accompanied only by another police officer, so answers C and D are incorrect. That officer may be from any police service, not necessarily the officer's own force and so answer B is incorrect. In relation to solicitors, at this stage of the proceedings the officer is not entitled to be legally represented in any case.

Question 7

Answer **C** — Part of the procedure under the Police (Efficiency) Regulations 1999 is to allow the member concerned, or the member of the police force who has accompanied him or both of them, an opportunity to make representations. As both are given the opportunity, answers A and B are incorrect. However, it is not mandatory for them to make these representations, which makes answer D incorrect.

Question 8

Answer **B** — The 'reasonable period' is normally not less than three months and no more than six months and therefore answers A, C and D are incorrect.

Question 9

Answer **A** — The notice must be sent not less than 21 days prior to the hearing and therefore answers B, C and D are incorrect.

Question 10

Answer **A** — Unlike the misconduct hearing, where the officer only has right to legal representation where the supervising officer has given written notice of that right (where various sanctions are being considered), in an inefficiency hearing the officer always has a right to legal representation and therefore answers C and D are incorrect. Although the officer must be sent a notice, which, amongst other things, outlines their right to representation, they always have this right and therefore answer B is incorrect. The difference lies in the fact that at an inefficiency hearing all sanctions, including dismissal are available and s. 84 of the Police Act 1996 allows representation where such a sanction is available. Misconduct hearings differ in that dismissal will not always be a sanction that is either available or appropriate.

Question 11

Answer **C** — Fairness and impartiality relates to even-handedness in dealing with the public and colleagues. There is no evidence the Sergeant is being 'unfair' to the officer, he may treat all his staff that way! Therefore answer A is incorrect. Abuse of authority relates to legal authority and not managerial authority and therefore answer C is incorrect. Performance of duties relates to performance of duties as a police officer and therefore answer D is incorrect. The term overbearing conduct towards a colleague, particularly to one junior in rank and service, is found in the Code of Conduct under politeness and tolerance.

Question 12

Answer **B** — One of the consequences of being suspended is that under the rules of the Police Promotion Examinations Board the officer will be unable to sit the qualifying examination. There is however an exception to this — answer A is therefore incorrect. Please note that the initial premise is that the suspended officer *cannot* take the examination and therefore answers C and D are incorrect. The exception is where the officer's chief officer has expressly authorised it.

Question 13

Answer **B** — There are certain complaints that are made against police officers that must be referred to the Police Complaints Authority. They are those involving death of, or serious injury to, some other person (which would include grievous bodily harm) and therefore answer D is incorrect. The requirement to refer also includes allegations of assault occasioning actual bodily harm, bribery or a serious arrestable offence. Therefore the minimum level of assault that requires mandatory referral is actual bodily harm (s. 47 of the Offences Against the Person Act 1861) and therefore answer A is incorrect. Although both grievous bodily harm offences would have to be referred, answer C is incorrect because it says 'at least' amounting to such harm, which if true would preclude actual bodily harm from referral.

Question 14

Answer **C** — A complaint, as defined in s. 65 of the Police Act 1996, must emanate from a member of the public and must be about the conduct of 'a member of a police force'. As special constables and cadets are not members of a police force, the definition does not apply to them and therefore answer A is incorrect. This is also true whether they are on or off duty and therefore answer B is incorrect. As far as special constables not being police officers is concerned, how could they perform duties if they did not have the appropriate powers, as all police officers have? Therefore answer D is also incorrect.

Question 15

Answer **C** — Impersonating a police officer is defined in the Police Act 1996. Section 90(1) states:

> *Any person who with intent to deceive impersonates a member of a police force or special constable, or makes any statement or does any act calculated falsely to suggest that he is such a member or constable shall be guilty of an offence . . .*

As can be seen from the definition, the legislation applies to special constables and therefore answer B is incorrect. The offence includes not only statements but also acts that suggest he is a special constable. Such acts would include producing a false warrant card and therefore answer A is incorrect. This is a crime of 'specific' intent and intention to deceive must be proved, not just an intention to gain an advantage and therefore answer D is incorrect.

Question 16

Answer **A** — In relation to sobriety, Home Office guidance suggests that Superintendents will be classed as being 'on duty' while they are formally on-call. They will not, however, be on duty by reason only of their general 24 hour responsibility and therefore answer C is incorrect. The guidance further provides that an officer who is *unexpectedly* called out for duty should be able, at no risk of discredit, to say that he or she has had too much to drink. That standard would be applied by the officer, and is not conditional on their being drunk and therefore answer D is incorrect. It would appear to be a prudent decision, not to attend a firearms incident having consumed intoxicating liquor, so it is certainly not unsatisfactory performance and answer B is incorrect.

2 HUMAN RIGHTS

STUDY PREPARATION

It is generally accepted that the introduction of the Human Rights Act 1998 (which incorporates the European Convention on Human Rights into our domestic law) has had the largest effect on the use of police powers since the Police and Criminal Evidence Act 1984 came into being. Many of the questions contained in this chapter are based on decisions made in the European Court of Human Rights. It remains to be seen how quickly such decisions will continue to be interpreted in England and Wales, as no doubt they will be challenged and developed regularly. Under s. 2 of the Human Rights Act 1998, courts and tribunals are under an obligation to take such decisions into account. However, it is important to remember that the Convention, as a 'living instrument' is constantly evolving.

When looking at the Convention rights in detail, it is also important to recognise the difference between an *absolute* right under the Convention (such as the right to freedom from torture under Article 3), and a *qualified* or *restricted* right, (such as Article 5, the right to liberty). Probably, the most important consideration is to recognise how the 1998 Act sets out to *balance* the rights of the individual against the needs of a democratic society.

The 'three tests' must be learned, namely 'prescribed by law', 'legitimate objective' and 'proportionality', as well as who will be a 'victim' and who may be in breach of the Act.

Lastly, there are several Articles contained in the Convention which directly affect the police, such as the right to life, freedom from torture, right to liberty and security, right to a fair trial and privacy.

Other Articles, such as right of freedom of expression and freedom of assembly also have a significant effect on everyday policing.

Human rights law does not exist in isolation. Therefore, although it is specifically addressed in this chapter, every aspect of the law contained in this book should be viewed with the 1998 Act in mind.

QUESTIONS

Question 1

In relation to whether courts in England and Wales should follow decisions made in the European Court of Human Rights, which of the following statements will be true?

[A] Any decision made in the European Court of Human Rights must be followed by courts in England and Wales.

[B] Courts in England and Wales need only take into account past cases from the European Court of Human Rights.

[C] Courts in England and Wales need not take into account past cases from the European Court of Human Rights.

[D] Courts in England and Wales must take into account cases from the European Court of Human Rights, but they need not follow them.

Question 2

In relation to a person's human rights being infringed which, if either, of the following statements is/are true?

1. Common law may not be used as a legal source to justify the actions of a public authority.
2. Provided its actions were proportionate, a public authority need not point to a legal source to justify its actions.

[A] Statement 1 only;

[B] Statement 2 only.

[C] Both statements.

[D] Neither statement.

Question 3

CARTWRIGHT is appearing in the Crown Court to appeal against his conviction for obstructing a police officer. He is alleged to have given misleading information to a police officer, as to who was driving his motor vehicle at the time of a road traffic accident. CARTWRIGHT believes that his appeal is justified, as the officer's questions were an infringement of his human rights. The alleged offence of obstruction occurred in September 2000.

In relation to CARTWRIGHT seeking a remedy under the Human Rights Act 1998, which of the following statements would be correct?

[A] He may not do so, as the alleged offence took place more than one year ago.

[B] He may do so, as the alleged offence took place less than three years ago.

[C] He may do so, regardless of how long ago the incident took place.

[D] He may not do so; the only way to use the Act is to institute proceedings against a public authority.

Question 4

The police are conducting observations near a lay-by, which is a meeting place for gay men. They are seeking to detect offences of homosexual activity in public, under the Sexual Offences Act 1956. DANE regularly frequents the area, and is also a member of a gay and lesbian group. He has sought legal advice in order to challenge police action under the Human Rights Act 1998.

In relation to whether DANE may use the Act to challenge the police activity, which statement is correct?

[A] He may do so as an individual only, whether he has been arrested or not.

[B] He may do so as part of a group, but only if he has been arrested for an offence.

[C] He may do so as part of a group, or as an individual, whether he has been arrested or not.

[D] He may do so as an individual only if he has been proceeded against for an offence.

Question 5

Article 2 of the European Convention on Human Rights relates to the protection of a person's right to life. In relation to the level of force that may legitimately be used when a life is taken in breach of this Article, which of the following statements is correct?

[A] No more force than is necessary in the circumstances may be used.
[B] No more force than is reasonable in the circumstances may be used.
[C] No more force than is absolutely necessary may be used.
[D] No more force than would appear necessary to a reasonable person may be used.

Question 6

LAWTON was the father of an eight-year-old boy, who was murdered by his neighbour PEARSON, a convicted sex offender. Prior to the murder, LAWTON had made several complaints to the police that PEARSON had been seen pestering his child. Following PEARSON's conviction, LAWTON brought an action against the police under Article 2 of the European Convention on Human Rights, alleging that the police had failed to prevent his son's death. LAWTON must prove that the police failed to take 'reasonable measures' that were in their powers to avoid the risk.

How would the court approach the issue of whether 'reasonable measures' were taken?

[A] By reference to the opinion of an objective third party.
[B] On the balance of probabilities, as to what risk the police actually foresaw.
[C] Beyond reasonable doubt, as to what risk the police actually foresaw.
[D] By reference to the subjective opinion of the police officer(s) involved in the decisions.

Question 7

HART works as a prison officer in a private prison. On several occasions GRANGER, a prisoner, had been rude to her. In order to teach GRANGER a lesson, HART made GRANGER stand in the shower for a whole hour, while she looked on.

Have GRANGER's rights been breached under Article 3 of the European Convention on Human Rights (right to freedom from torture)?

[A] No, because HART does not work for a public authority.
[B] Yes, because HART's employer performs a public function.
[C] No, because HART does not work for a government authority.
[D] Yes, regardless of the employer that HART works for.

Question 8

In relation to the provisions of Article 3 of the European Convention on Human Rights (right to freedom from torture), which of the following statements, if either, is/are correct?

1. Article 3 provides a statutory defence of 'lawful authority, justification or excuse'.
2. Words alone could constitute inhuman and degrading treatment under Article 3.

[A] Statement 1 only.
[B] Statement 2 only.
[C] Both statements.
[D] Neither statement.

Question 9

Constable WILSON was called to an incident in a local supermarket. The manager was complaining about SHEPPARD, who was homeless. SHEPPARD had entered the store and told the manager that he had scabies and a severe lice infection that were highly contagious and needed treatment. The manager feared that customers and staff would be infected by disease and requested that the officer removed SHEPPARD from the store.

What power does Article 5 of the European Convention on Human Rights (the right to liberty and security) provide in relation to an arrest under these circumstances?

[A] SHEPPARD can be arrested, provided he is taken to a medical centre.
[B] SHEPPARD can be arrested and taken to a place of safety.
[C] SHEPPARD cannot be arrested under the Convention, the officer would need to seek powers from elsewhere.
[D] SHEPPARD can be arrested and brought before a competent legal authority.

Question 10

In relation to the provisions of Article 5 of the European Convention on Human Rights (the right to liberty and security), which, if either, of the following statements is/are correct?

1. A minor for the purposes of Article 5 will be a person who has not attained the age of 18.
2. A person who has been unlawfully detained has a right to compensation under Article 5, but this right does not extend to suing a court.

[A] Statement 1 only.
[B] Statement 2 only.
[C] Both statements.
[D] Neither statement.

Question 11

Constable OSBORN has been charged with an internal discipline offence arising from the performance of his duties. He was interviewed by a senior police officer, but was not allowed to have a legal representative present. He is due to appear before a Police Conduct hearing and is seeking advice as to how the Human Rights Act 1998 affects his treatment and those proceedings.

In relation to Article 6 of the European Convention on Human Rights (the right to a fair trial), which of the following statements is correct?

[A] Article 6 applies to court cases only; therefore the disciplinary proceedings are not affected.
[B] Article 6 applies to all disciplinary hearings and OSBORN's rights appear to have been infringed by the failure to allow him access to a solicitor.
[C] Article 6 applies to purely criminal cases only; therefore OSBORN's rights have not been infringed, and the proceedings are not affected.
[D] Article 6 applies to some disciplinary hearings; however, OSBORN's rights have not been infringed by denying him access to a solicitor.

Question 12

BRACE owns 15 private children's nurseries, each of which is managed separately by his employees. BRACE has computerised records dating back several years of applicants for posts in his nurseries. Amongst these records are details of people whom he considers are unsuitable for work with children.

Would the people on the list be able to bring proceedings against BRACE under Article 8 of the European Convention on Human Rights (right to a private life) in these circumstances?

[A] Yes, he is in breach of the human rights of the people on the list.
[B] No, he could claim a pressing social need to maintain the list.
[C] No, because the list is not being maintained by a public authority.
[D] Yes, because he could not point to a lawful authority enabling him to maintain the list.

Question 13

CLAYTON is appearing in the Crown Court, having been charged with an offence of stirring up racial hatred under s. 18 of the Public Order Act 1986. He had displayed a picture in his shop window, indicating that he would not serve refugees. He is pleading not guilty, claiming that his human rights have been interfered with, as he is entitled to express his opinions freely.

Would CLAYTON be able to use Article 10 of the European Convention on Human Rights (freedom of expression) as a defence in these circumstances?

[A] No, as his actions are probably not proportionate to the crime committed.
[B] Yes, every person has a right to express themselves freely.
[C] No, but he could use Article 9 (freedom of thought) as a defence.
[D] Yes, provided he held a genuine belief that his rights had been interfered with.

Question 14

The Westford anti-hunt lobby arranged a demonstration outside a farm where a fox hunt was being organised. The organisers of the hunt arranged for marshals to be present and the local police were also in attendance. Demonstrators protested peacefully in the road nearby but, on the instructions of the hunt organisers, the marshals attempted to move the protestors away from the scene. The demonstrators felt intimidated by the marshals, but the police did nothing.

In these circumstances, do the police officers at the scene appear to have infringed Article 11 of the European Convention on Human Rights (freedom of assembly)?

[A] No, as they have not interfered with the rights of the protestors or the members of the hunt.
[B] Yes, they should have stopped the protest; it breached the rights of the hunters and the farm owner.
[C] Yes, they had a duty to prevent the unlawful interference with the rights of the protestors by the marshals.
[D] No, they would only have a duty to act if public order offences were imminent.

ANSWERS

Question 1

Answer **D** — Under s. 2 of the Human Rights Act 1998, the courts of England and Wales have a duty to take into account *any* decision made in the European Court of Human Rights and therefore answers B and C are incorrect. However, there is no stipulation that the courts of England and Wales must follow the decisions, merely that they take decisions into account and therefore answer A is incorrect.

Question 2

Answer **D** — Both statements are incorrect. Any infringement of a person's human rights must be prescribed by law, for a legitimate objective and be proportional (the three tests).

Dealing with statement 2 first, any interference with a person's Convention rights *must* be traceable to a clear legal source (i.e. the source of a public body's authority to act lawfully). Therefore, a public body's actions must be both proportional *and* lawful, (and aimed towards a legitimate objective). Therefore answers B and C are incorrect.

In relation to statement 1, the source of law must be clearly and precisely defined and publicised, so that people have the opportunity to behave accordingly. A statutory rule will meet this requirement, as will the common law, if sufficiently clear. Answer A is therefore incorrect.

Question 3

Answer **C** — A person may use the Human Rights Act 1998 either to bring proceedings against a public authority, *or* to use the Act as a defence to their actions against a public authority. The first method is known as using the legislation as a sword and the second is known as using the Act as a shield. A person may also use a public authority's actions as grounds for judicial review (using as a sword). Answer D is incorrect as a person may use the Act in their defence.

Under s. 7 of the 1998 Act, any proceedings against a public authority must be brought within one year from the date the incident complained of took place. The time limit, however, *does not* apply where a person is using the Act as a 'shield' in court proceedings (which is why answers A and B are incorrect).

Therefore, regardless of whether Cartwright has a legitimate appeal, he may attempt to use the Human Rights Act 1998 to acquit himself.

Question 4

Answer **A** — Under s. 7(1) of the Human Rights Act 1998, a person who claims that a public authority has acted (or proposed to act) in a way that is incompatible with their human rights (s. 6(1)), may bring proceedings against the authority in the appropriate court or tribunal.

In order to rely on s. 7, however, a person must first be a 'victim', and must show that they are either *directly affected* or *at risk of being directly affected*. Section 7 will not enable public interest groups to institute proceedings, only individuals and therefore answers B and C are incorrect.

Answer A is correct because Dane is an individual who is at risk of being directly affected. The circumstances are similar to the case of *Dudgeon* v *United Kingdom* (1981) 4 EHRR 149, where the petitioner was able to challenge the law proscribing consensual homosexual activity even though he had not been prosecuted under the legislation himself. A person may institute proceedings under s. 7 regardless of whether or not they have been convicted of an offence. This is known as using the European Convention on Human Rights as a 'sword' against a public authority.

Of course, whether the police should have been engaged in such surveillance, bearing in mind the Regulation of Investigatory Powers Act 2000, is another issue!

Question 5

Answer **C** — The term 'reasonable force' does not apply to the application of lethal force under the Human Rights Act 1998, making answers B and D incorrect.

Answer A is close; however, the Act states that when life is taken, any force used must be shown to have been *no more than absolutely necessary* (which is why C is correct).

Question 6

Answer **A** — The circumstances are similar to those from the case of *Osman* v *United Kingdom* (2000) 29 EHRR 245, where a man had been killed by a person who had become fixated with him. The Court took the view that it is possible for an individual to show that the State had violated Article 2 by failing to protect his or her right to life under certain circumstances. In order to do so, it would seem that the person must show:

- that the police knew/ought to have known
- of the existence of a real and immediate risk
- to the life/lives of identified individual(s)
- presented by the criminal acts of another

and the police failed to take reasonable measures that were within their powers to avoid that risk.

'Reasonable measures' in such a case would be judged objectively, that is, by reference to the opinion of an objective third party and not the subjective opinion of the police officer(s) concerned in the decision.

Answer A is a direct quote from the *Osman* ruling, which is why answers B, C and D are incorrect.

Question 7

Answer **B** — Under Article 3 of the European Convention on Human Rights a person must not be subjected to torture, inhuman or degrading treatment or punishment. Therefore, the actions of the guard would amount to a breach.

Under s. 6 of the Human Rights Act 1998, it is unlawful for a public authority to act in a way that is incompatible with a Convention right. An individual working for an authority is included in the definition.

'Public authorities' are divided into 'pure public authorities' (such as the police and courts etc.); and 'quasi-public authorities'. There has been no test as yet as to who might fall under the second category, but they *do* include authorities who have a duty to discharge *some* public duties (such as security companies running private prisons and government contractors). Therefore, answer A is incorrect.

Answer C is incorrect because 'government authorities' are not mentioned and answer D is incorrect, as regard *must* be given to the type of authority a person works for.

Question 8

Answer **B** — Although torture is a specific criminal offence under s. 134 of the Criminal Justice Act 1988, with a statutory defence of 'lawful authority, justification or excuse', the prohibition contained in Article 3 of the European Convention on Human Rights is *absolute.* Irrespective of the prevailing circumstances, there can be no derogation from an individual's absolute right to freedom from torture, inhuman or degrading treatment or punishment. Statement 1 is incorrect for this reason and therefore answers A and C are incorrect.

In the case of *Denmark* v *Greece* (1969) 12 YB Eur Conv HR special vol., it was held that causing mental anguish without any physical assault could be a violation of Article 3. It is likely that courts within the United Kingdom would accept that words alone might amount to inhuman or degrading treatment, making statement 2 correct and therefore answer D incorrect.

Question 9

Answer **C** — Under Article 5 of the European Convention on Human Rights, every person has the right to liberty and security of person. This is a qualified right, and exceptions are provided in Article 5(1), allowing the lawful arrest in certain cases, where the procedure is prescribed by law.

Article 5(1)(e) provides that a person may be detained without their human rights being infringed where their detention is necessary 'for the prevention of the spreading of infectious diseases, of persons of unsound mind, alcoholics or drug addicts or vagrants'.

However, the Convention itself *does not* provide a specific power of arrest for the above offences and arresting officers would have to rely on existing legislation to detain a person (which is why answer C is correct and answers A, B and D are incorrect).

Article 5(1) merely sets out the conditions under which the State may remove a person's liberty. (In real terms, it is hard to imagine that the legislators intended to provide a power to arrest all people with infectious diseases, drug addicts, alcoholics and vagrants!)

Question 10

Answer **A** — Statement 1 is correct; a minor under Article 5 of the European Convention on Human Rights is a person under the age of 18 years.

A person who has been unlawfully detained has a right to compensation under Article 5, and this right *does* extend to suing a court, as the right applies to the people concerned in the arrest/detention *and* the court where appropriate (making statement 2 incorrect). Consequently, answers B, C and D are incorrect.

Question 11

Answer **D** — Article 6 of the European Convention on Human Rights Act has been held to apply to some professional and disciplinary hearings, and it is possible that it will affect police disciplinary hearings (answers A and C are incorrect for this reason).

However, it was held in the case of *Lee v United Kingdom* (2000) LTL 22 September, that where an officer was interviewed for a *purely disciplinary* matter, there was no standing right of access to a lawyer, even if he or she were being interviewed under caution. This decision can be interpreted as meaning that the officer was not being interviewed for an 'offence', and would therefore not enjoy the usual right to legal representation under the Police and Criminal Evidence Act 1984 that he or she would otherwise have had. Since the matter was an internal police investigation, the officer would not be entitled to legal representation, even if he or she were authorised before the interview (making answer B incorrect).

Question 12

Answer **C** — Article 8 of the European Convention on Human Rights states that everyone has the right to respect for his private life, his home and his correspondence. However, the Human Rights Act 1998 aims to protect people from the arbitrary interference by 'public authorities'. Therefore, even though it might seem that Brace is acting contrary to the Convention, the list of names is not maintained by a public authority (which is why answer C is correct).

Had Brace been acting on behalf of a public authority, he would probably still be protected, because of the case of *R v Worcester County Council, ex parte W* [2000] 1 FLR 406. Here, it was decided that the Consultancy Services Index maintained by the Secretary of

State, which provided access to employers' records on people considered unsuitable for work with children, was not an infringement of the human rights of those included on it. It has also been held that maintaining such a list is proportionate to the lawful objective sought (*R* v *Secretary of State for Health, ex parte L (M)* [2001] 1 FLR 406). Answers A, B and D are incorrect for this reason.

Question 13

Answer **A** — Under Article 10 of the European Convention on Human Rights, everyone has a right to freedom of expression. However, as with all aspects of human rights, this has to be balanced against other social needs. In the case of *Hutchinson* v *DPP, The Independent,* 20 November 2000, a conviction for criminal damage was upheld when it was decided that there were other ways in which the defendant could have expressed her opinions without committing a crime. Answer B is incorrect for this reason.

Because his actions were probably not proportionate, Clayton would not be able to use Article 9 as a 'shield' for the same reasons as above (making answer C incorrect).

A person's belief, no matter how genuine, that their rights had been interfered with, will not provide an automatic defence to a criminal offence, if that belief is not proportionate to the crime committed. Answer D is therefore incorrect.

Question 14

Answer **C** — Under Article 11 of the European Convention on Human Rights, everyone has the right to freedom of *peaceful assembly.* Therefore, the protestors had the right to protest, provided they were going about it peacefully. They do not appear to have interfered with the rights of the members of the hunt or the farm owner on these facts. Answer B is incorrect for this reason.

The State (or public authority) has two main obligations in these circumstances. In the first instance, they must not interfere with the protestors' rights to peaceful assembly. However, equally as important, they have a *positive duty to prevent others* from interfering with that right (which is why answer C is correct).

Therefore, even though the officers at the scene did not actively prevent the protest, arguably they should have acted to stop the marshals from doing so (which is why answers A and D are incorrect).

3 POLICE POWERS

The areas covered in this chapter could hardly be more important. In practical terms, this chapter contains the police officer's tool kit — and if it is relevant in practice, it is highly relevant in preparing for an examination or course of study.

In deciding what to do in any given situation, it is vital that you know what you are *empowered* to do. Following on from the previous chapter, it is also important to realise that each police power equals a reduction of, or interference with someone's human rights. As holders of such powers, police officers are under a duty to exercise them properly — lawfully, proportionately and fairly.

The main tools in the bag are powers of entry, arrest, search and seizure. Some are very broadly based (such as arrestable offences) while others are contextual, requiring very specific circumstances to exist first before they are available. Knowing and understanding all of these lead to confidence, not just as a student or exam candidate but as a police officer generally.

QUESTIONS

Question 1

Section 107 of the Police and Criminal Evidence Act 1984 refers to officers performing duties in acting ranks. In relation to s. 107, under which circumstances would a constable be able to perform the functions of a custody officer at a designated police station?

[A]   When he or she has been authorised to do so by an Inspector.
[B]   When he or she has been authorised to do so by a Superintendent.
[C]   When no other custody officer is readily available.
[D]   When he or she has been temporarily promoted to Sergeant.

Question 2

Constable AMIR was on patrol looking for a person who had committed theft from a vehicle. Witnesses had given a description of the person responsible, who they said was carrying a screwdriver. Constable AMIR discovered JACKSON, who matched the description, in the front garden of a house. JACKSON lived some three miles away from the house.

Would Constable AMIR have the power to search JACKSON for the screwdriver in these circumstances?

[A]   No, as JACKSON was in the garden of a dwelling.
[B]   Yes, as JACKSON was not inside a dwelling.
[C]   No, as JACKSON was not in a public place.
[D]   Yes, as JACKSON was not in his own garden.

Question 3

Under s. 3 of the Police and Criminal Evidence Act 1984, a constable is required to make a record following a search conducted under s. 1 of the Act.

In relation to the records required, which of the following statements, if either, is/are correct?

1. A failure by a constable to make a record would not render the search itself unlawful.
2. If the officer does not know the person's name, he or she may detain the person in order to find out.

[A] Statement 1 only.
[B] Statement 2 only.
[C] Both statements.
[D] Neither statement.

Question 4

Constable ROBERTS attended a large retail store, where the occupants of a green 4X4 vehicle had been captured on CCTV as they entered the store and stole two bottles of wine from within. The vehicle was seen to make off immediately prior to PC ROBERTS' arrival. PC ROBERTS contacted the control room and asked the duty Sergeant to authorise an urgent road check, under s. 4 of the Police and Criminal Evidence Act 1984, for the vehicle and its occupants.

Can the officer's request be granted in these circumstances?

[A] Yes, but Constable ROBERTS could have authorised the road check himself.
[B] No, a road check may not be authorised in these circumstances.
[C] No, only an Inspector may authorise a road check in urgent circumstances.
[D] No, only a Superintendent may authorise a road check.

Question 5

Section 4 of the Police and Criminal Evidence Act 1984 requires the police to provide a written statement when a motor vehicle has been stopped during a road check.

Who would be entitled to apply for such a statement?

[A] The person in charge of the vehicle at the time it was stopped.
[B] The owner of the vehicle at the time it was stopped.
[C] The driver of the vehicle at the time it was stopped.
[D] Any person who was in the vehicle at the time it was stopped.

Question 6

A football match is due to take place in Inspector CARTER's area, and she is the officer in charge of a Support Unit positioned outside the train station. Intelligence has suggested that approximately 200 away supporters will be arriving, and staff on the train have reported seeing several weapons being carried by fans. Inspector CARTER is considering searching all supporters before they leave the train station.

In relation to the powers to authorise searches under s. 60 of the Criminal Justice and Public Order Act 1994, which statement is correct?

[A] The Inspector may authorise the searches, but only if she suspects there will be incidents involving serious violence.
[B] The Inspector may authorise the searches, but only of those suspected of carrying weapons.
[C] The Inspector may authorise the search of any of the fans, in these circumstances alone.
[D] The Inspector may not authorise the searches, this power is restricted to Superintendents.

Question 7

Constable WILLIS was on patrol in the early hours of the morning, searching for two teenagers suspected of burglary of a shop. The teenagers had been seen on CCTV, and both were wearing ski masks. Constable WILLIS found HALL and SULLIVAN nearby; HALL was wearing a ski mask, SULLIVAN was not.

What power would Constable WILLIS have to deal with HALL and SULLIVAN under s. 60(4A) of the Criminal Justice and Public Order Act 1994?

[A] He has no power to deal with either person under this Act.
[B] To demand the removal of HALL's mask, and search SULLIVAN.
[C] To search SULLIVAN, but not to demand the removal of HALL's mask.
[D] To demand the removal of HALL's mask, but not to search SULLIVAN.

Question 8

Section 33 of the Terrorism Act 2000 empowers the police to set up cordons if it is considered expedient to do so for the purposes of a terrorist investigation. In relation to the 2000 Act, which of the following statements, if either, is/are correct?

1. A constable may make a designation under the Act if it is a matter of urgency.
2. An initial designation under the Act cannot extend beyond seven days from the time the order is made.

[A] Statement 1 only.
[B] Statement 2 only.
[C] Both statements.
[D] Neither statement.

Question 9

Section 28 of the Police and Criminal Evidence Act 1984 provides that a person must be informed if he/she is under arrest and also of the grounds for his/her arrest.

Which statement below accurately describes the circumstances where a person need not be informed of these facts?

[A] Where it is impracticable because of the person's condition.
[B] Where it is impracticable because a person has escaped from arrest.
[C] Where it is impracticable because of the person's behaviour.
[D] Where it is impracticable because of the person's condition or behaviour.

Question 10

POINTER entered an off licence with another man and they stood near the wine display. The two left without buying anything. However, the owner, STROUD, noticed that three bottles of wine were missing. STROUD checked the CCTV, which showed POINTER and the other man removing the bottles of wine, but they had their backs to the camera and it was unclear which of the two had actually taken the wine. STROUD had placed the bottles on display before the men had entered the shop and no other customers had been in since that time. STROUD saw POINTER alone in the street the next day.

Does STROUD have a power to arrest POINTER for theft in these circumstances?

[A] No, POINTER would have to be in the act of committing an arrestable offence.
[B] No, STROUD would have to know that POINTER was guilty of an arrestable offence before he could arrest him.
[C] No, STROUD would have to be a police officer to arrest POINTER in these circumstances.
[D] Yes, provided STROUD had reasonable grounds to suspect that POINTER was guilty of theft.

Question 11

Section 25 of the Police and Criminal Evidence Act 1984 describes circumstances under which a constable may arrest a person using the general arrest conditions.

Under which of the following circumstances, would a constable be entitled to arrest a person who has provided their name?

[A] Where the constable has reasonable grounds for suspecting that the person has not given his or her real name.

[B] Where the constable knows that the person has not given his or her real name.

[C] Where the constable has reasonable grounds for believing that the person has not given his or her real name.

[D] Where the constable has reasonable grounds for doubting that the person has given his or her real name.

Question 12

Authority is provided to deal with all military personnel, who have been arrested as deserters or absentees. In relation to the powers provided, which of the following statements is correct?

[A] An absentee or deserter must be taken directly to the nearest appropriate military establishment on arrest.

[B] An absentee or deserter must be taken directly to a magistrates' court on arrest, to be dealt with accordingly.

[C] An absentee or deserter must be taken directly to a police station on arrest, to await the arrival of the appropriate military personnel.

[D] An absentee must be taken directly to a police station on arrest, however a deserter must be taken to a magistrates' court.

Question 13

WEAVER was reported for an offence of driving without insurance. He failed to appear at court and the case was heard in his absence. WEAVER already had 10 points on his driving licence, and the magistrate ruled that he should receive a disqualification. Summonses had been served on WEAVER at his home address and the prosecuting solicitor submitted that the court should issue a warrant for his arrest to appear in court.

Would the magistrate be able to issue an arrest warrant in these circumstances to secure WEAVER's attendance in court?

[A] No, a court may not issue a warrant when a person has only committed a summary offence.
[B] No, a court may only issue a warrant when a person has committed an imprisonable offence.
[C] Yes, a court may issue a warrant when it intends to disqualify a person from driving.
[D] No, the court may only issue a warrant for a summary offence when the defendant's name and address is not known.

Question 14

Which of the following warrants would need to be in the possession of the officer when being executed?

1. A warrant issued in connection with domestic proceedings.
2. A warrant issued for non-payment of fines.

[A] Warrant 1 only.
[B] Warrant 2 only.
[C] Both warrants.
[D] Neither warrant.

Question 15

Constable SAVASTANO was on duty at 4.00 am. She was stopped by PEARSON, who reported that he had just seen several men taking electrical equipment into his neighbour's house. An intelligence system check revealed that the occupier of the house had previous convictions for burglary and that stolen property had been found in his house in the past. Constable SAVASTANO was considering applying for a warrant to search the premises, so that evidence was not lost. However, she discovered that the duty Inspector had gone home feeling ill.

In relation to Constable SAVASTANO's application for a warrant in these circumstances, which of the following statements is correct?

[A]   Only an Inspector may authorise the application.
[B]   The most senior officer on duty may authorise the application.
[C]   Any constable may authorise the application.
[D]   Only a Sergeant may authorise the application.

Question 16

Section 16 of the Police and Criminal Evidence Act 1984 deals with the execution of search warrants.

In relation to s. 16, which of the following statements, if either, is/are true?

1.   A search warrant must be executed within 30 days of its issue.
2.   If the occupier of premises is absent when a search warrant is executed, it must be posted to him or her within one month of the search.

[A]   Statement 1 only.
[B]   Statement 2 only.
[C]   Both statements.
[D]   Neither statement.

Question 17

Constable AHMED has arrested GRANT for an offence of taking a vehicle without the owner's consent. Constable AHMED has been advised to seek permission from the duty Inspector to search GRANT's home address, under s. 18 of the Police and Criminal Evidence Act 1984.

In relation to where Constable AHMED may search, and what he may search for, which of the following statements is correct?

[A]   Premises occupied or controlled by GRANT, for evidence related to the offence for which he is in custody, or another similar arrestable offence.

[B]   Premises suspected to be occupied or controlled by GRANT, for evidence related to the offence he is in custody for, or other similar arrestable offences.

[C]   Premises occupied or controlled by GRANT, for evidence related to the offence for which he is in custody only.

[D]   Premises occupied or controlled by GRANT, for evidence related to the offence for which he is in custody, or any other arrestable offence.

Question 18

Constable WILSON attended a burglary in the early hours of the morning. A witness, COLE, had seen a man breaking into a shop and removing two video recorders. COLE saw the man enter a house next to the shop. A short while later COLE saw the same man emerge empty handed and walk up the street. Constable WILSON made a search of the area and arrested GREEN, who matched the description given, nearby within minutes.

Constable WILSON considered searching the house GREEN had been seen entering. What authority would she have to do so in these circumstances?

[A] She has no authority to search immediately, and would have to seek permission under s. 18 of the Police and Criminal Evidence Act 1984.

[B] She would have authority to search any premises which GREEN was in at any time prior to his arrest under s. 32 of the Police and Criminal Evidence Act 1984.

[C] She would have authority to search any premises which GREEN was in immediately prior to his arrest under s. 32 of the Police and Criminal Evidence Act 1984.

[D] She would have authority to search any premises occupied or controlled by GREEN and which he was in immediately prior to his arrest under s. 32 of the Police and Criminal Evidence Act 1984.

Question 19

In which of the following circumstances, if any, may a constable enter premises using powers under s. 17 of the Police and Criminal Evidence Act 1984?

1. In order to prevent any criminal damage being caused to property.
2. To arrest a person whom he or she is pursuing, who is subject of an order under the Mental Health Act 1983.

[A] Circumstance 1 only.
[B] Circumstance 2 only.
[C] Both circumstances.
[D] Neither circumstance.

Question 20

HUDSON was arrested by Constable BALL from the Stolen Vehicle Squad, following the execution of a warrant at HUDSON'S garage, where several stolen vehicles were found. Constable BALL received intelligence that HUDSON had another vehicle, which was parked outside his house. Constable BALL suspected that this vehicle might also be stolen.

In relation to searching and seizing the vehicle or its contents under ss. 18 and 19 of the Police and Criminal Evidence Act 1984, what powers would be available to Constable BALL?

[A] The vehicle is 'premises', which cannot seized; the officer may search it and seize any contents obtained as a consequence of the commission of an offence.

[B] The vehicle is not 'premises' and may not be searched under s. 18; the officer would have to use powers available under s. 1 of the Act.

[C] The vehicle may be searched and seized if it is suspected it was obtained as a consequence of the commission of an offence, or for intelligence purposes.

[D] The vehicle and its contents may be searched and seized if it is suspected it was obtained as a consequence of the commission of an offence.

ANSWERS

Question 1

Answer **C** — Under s. 107(4), an officer of any rank may perform the functions of a custody officer at a designated police station if a custody officer is not readily available to perform them. However, the case of *Vince and Another* v *Chief Constable of Dorset Police* [1993] 1 WLR 415, made it clear that this should only be an exception.

Custody officers should be appointed, and will, according to s. 107(3), be of at least the rank of Sergeant.

There is nothing in s. 107(4) stating that a person performing the function in these circumstances must be authorised. There is also no requirement for the person to be temporarily promoted (which is why answers A, B and D are incorrect).

Question 2

Answer **D** — Powers to stop, search and seize are essentially intended for use in public places, meaning places to which the public, or any section of the public, has access, on payment or otherwise, as of right or by virtue of express or implied permission, or any other place to which people have ready access at the time when it is proposed to exercise the powers but which is not a dwelling (s. 1(1)(a) and (b) of the Police and Criminal Evidence Act 1984).

However, although powers to stop and search may not be exercised in a dwelling house, they may be exercised in a garden or yard of a house (s. 1(4) and (5)), provided it is *not* the person's own garden, and the officer has reasonable grounds for believing that he or she does not have permission (express or implied), to be there.

Therefore, although the search could not take place under s. 1(1)(b), the officer may use powers available under s. 1(4) and (5), as JACK-SON was not in his own garden. For these reasons answers A, B and C are incorrect.

Question 3

Answer **A** — It has been held that a failure to make a record of a search *does not* thereby render the search unlawful (*Basher* v *DPP* [1993] COD 372). Therefore statement 1 is correct.

The search record should contain the person's name but, if the officer does not know the name of the person, he or she *cannot detain* that person simply to find it out (s. 3(3) of the Police and Criminal Evidence Act 1984) and a description should be recorded instead (s. 3(4)). Therefore statement 2 is incorrect. Consequently, answers B, C and D are incorrect.

Question 4

Answer **B** — Section 4 of the Police and Criminal Evidence Act 1984 states that a road check may only be authorised where the officer has reasonable grounds for believing that the offence committed is a *serious arrestable offence*. Therefore, as the offence is one of shoplifting, a road check may not be authorised in the given circumstances, and answer B is the only possible correct answer.

In the case of a serious arrestable offence, the authorising officer may be below the rank of Superintendent and in this case could have been Constable ROBERTS (which would have made answer A correct).

Answer C is incorrect, as the 1984 Act does not specify any particular officer below the rank of Superintendent for urgent authorisations, and answer D is incorrect for the above reasons.

Question 5

Answer **A** — Under s. 4 of the Police and Criminal Evidence Act 1984, where a vehicle has been stopped during a road check, the *person in charge* of the vehicle is entitled to a written statement of the purpose of the check, if he or she applies no later than 12 months from the time the vehicle was stopped. Consequently, answers B, C and D are incorrect.

Question 6

Answer **C** — Under s. 60 of the Police and Criminal Evidence Act, if an Inspector reasonably believes that incidents of serious violence may take place in his/her area *or* that people are carrying dangerous instruments or offensive weapons, he or she may give an authorisation to stop any pedestrian and search him for offensive weapons or dangerous instruments.

The power used to be restricted to Superintendents, but may now be exercised by an Inspector (which is why answer D is incorrect).

The authorisation may be given either for incidents of serious violence *or* to search for weapons (making answer A incorrect). The power is to search any pedestrian, and is not restricted to those who may be carrying weapons (which is why answer B is incorrect).

Question 7

Answer **A** — Section 60(4A) of the Criminal Justice and Public Order Act 1994 allows the removal of items concealing identity, *but only where authorisation has been given under s. 60 of the Act.* Clearly, no such authorisation has been given in these circumstances (which is why answer A is the only possible correct answer and answers B, C and D are incorrect).

Had an authorisation been given under s. 60, the officer would have been able to require the removal of HALL's mask, but would not have been able to search SULLIVAN as no power is provided to do so. (There would obviously have been a power to search under s. 1 of the Police and Criminal Evidence Act 1984). There is a power of arrest should a person fail to remove an article.

Question 8

Answer **A** — Section 33 of the Terrorism Act 2000 deals with the power to cordon off areas to assist in terrorist investigations. Under s. 33(1), the authorisation or designation will be made by a Superintendent. However, under s. 34(2), a constable who is not of the rank required by subsection (1) may make a designation if he or she considers it necessary by reason of urgency. (This makes statement 1 correct).

The initial designation cannot extend beyond *14* days from the time the order is made (s. 35(2)). (This makes statement 2 incorrect). This period may be extended to a maximum period of 28 days.

Question 9

Answer **B** — The exception from a person being informed of arrest, provided under s. 28(5) of the Police and Criminal Evidence Act 1984, will only apply where: 'it was not reasonably practicable for him to be so informed by reason of his having escaped from arrest before the information could be given'. Therefore answer B is the only possible correct answer.

Answers A, C and D are taken from PACE Code of Practice, Code C, para. 10.3. Under this Code, a person need not be *cautioned* if it is impracticable to do so because of their condition or behaviour.

Question 10

Answer **D** — Under s. 24 of the Police and Criminal Evidence Act 1984, certain powers of arrest are provided for *any person*, while others are provided for police officers only.

Under s. 24(5) of the Act, where an arrestable offence has been committed, *any person* may arrest without warrant any person who is guilty of the offence *or* any person whom he has reasonable grounds for suspecting to be guilty of it.

An arrestable offence has been committed — theft of a bottle of wine. STROUD would have reasonable grounds for suspecting that POINTER had taken the wine, based on what he had seen on the video.

Answer A is incorrect because the power of arrest for any person is not restricted to those occasions where an arrestable offence is being committed.

Answer B is incorrect because s. 24(4) applies either when a person has committed an offence or where a person is reasonably suspected to have committed one, and is not restricted to police officers (making answer C incorrect).

Question 11

Answer **D** — Under s. 25(3)(b) of the Police and Criminal Evidence Act 1984, the officer must have 'reasonable grounds for doubting' that the name furnished by the relevant person is his or her real name. This would appear to be a very wide expression, and is not limited to suspecting that the name given is false and therefore answers A, B and C are incorrect.

This, together with the expression 'reasonable grounds for doubting' should be contrasted with the further general arrest conditions set out under s. 25(3)(d) and (e). The expression used there is a narrower one requiring the officer to have reasonable grounds to *believe* that the arrest is *necessary* — as opposed to simply desirable — in order to prevent the person from bringing about the consequences set out in those subsections.

Question 12

Answer **B** — A power of arrest is provided under the Army Act 1955, the Air Force Act 1955 and under the Navy Discipline Act 1957. An absentee or deserter must be taken directly to a magistrates' court and the appropriate service should be informed, therefore answers A, C and D are incorrect.

An absentee or deserter may be remanded in custody by the courts, to await escort, or if it is likely to be provided soon, to a police station.

Question 13

Answer **C** — Magistrates' courts can only issue a warrant for failing to appear at court where the offence is imprisonable *or* where they intend to impose a disqualification from holding a licence having convicted the defendant. This makes answer B incorrect.

They may generally issue an arrest warrant for offences that are imprisonable or indictable only or where the person's address is not sufficient for the service of a summons. This case does not involve an arrest warrant, which makes answers A and D incorrect.

Question 14

Answer **B** — Warrants issued in connection with 'an offence' (or for some purposes concerning the armed forces and domestic proceedings) do not need to be in the possession of the officer executing them at the time (s. 125 of the Magistrates' Courts Act 1980). As the warrant under statement 1 is not correct, as it does not need to be in possession, answers A, C and D are incorrect.

However, where the warrant is for non-payment of a fine, the officer must have the warrant with him or her as the defendant should have the opportunity to pay the outstanding amount (*R* v *Peacock* (1989) 153 JP 199).

Question 15

Answer **B** — Applications for all search warrants must be made with the authority of an officer of at least the rank of Inspector (PACE Code B, para. 2.4). However, in cases of urgency where no such officer is 'readily available', the senior officer on duty may authorise the application and therefore answers A, C and D are incorrect.

The case in question would seem suitable for the application of a warrant, as it is reasonable to suspect that stolen property was being taken into a house. The matter would probably be considered urgent, as it would be desirable to search the premises before the stolen property was moved.

Question 16

Answer **D** — Neither statement is true. Consequently, answers A, B and C are incorrect.

A search warrant must be executed within one calendar month of its issue. If there is no person present when a search warrant is executed, a copy of the warrant must be left in a prominent place on the premises.

Question 17

Answer **A** — Under s. 18 of the Police and Criminal Evidence Act 1984, a constable may enter and search any premises occupied or controlled by a person who is under arrest for an arrestable offence, if there are reasonable grounds to suspect that there are items on the premises that relate to that offence, *or* to some other arrestable offence which is connected with or similar to that offence.

Answer B is incorrect because the premises *must* be controlled or occupied by the person, it is not enough that the officer suspects or believes that they are.

Answers C and D are incorrect as the officer may search for evidence relating to either the offence for which the suspect has been arrested, or those which are similar.

Question 18

Answer **C** — Authority is provided under s. 32 of the Police and Criminal Evidence Act 1984 for a constable to enter and search any premises in which the person was when arrested or immediately before being arrested, if the constable has reasonable grounds for believing that there is evidence on the premises in consequence of the commission of an offence. As Cole had been in premises immediately before his arrest, the officer could use s. 32, answer A is therefore incorrect. The search may be conducted for the purpose of finding evidence relating to the offence for which the person was arrested. As the defendant in the scenario was arrested within minutes of leaving the premises, this would be classed as 'immediately' (although the term immediately is open to interpretation).

Answer B is incorrect as the search relates to premises the person was in *immediately* prior to arrest.

Answer D is incorrect, as s. 32 does not state that the premises must be one which is occupied or controlled by the person arrested. (This requirement may be found in s. 18 of the Act).

Question 19

Answer **B** — Section 17 of the Police and Criminal Evidence Act 1984 provides authority for a constable to enter premises to arrest a person in several circumstances.

Under s. 17(1)(e), a constable may enter premises for the purposes of saving life or limb, or preventing *serious damage* to property. The mere fact that a person is causing criminal damage would not be sufficient under this section (making circumstance 1 incorrect and answers A and C incorrect).

Under s. 17(1)(d), a constable may enter premises for the purposes of recapturing a person who is unlawfully at large, and whom he or she is pursuing. 'Unlawfully at large' will include a person who is subject of an order under the Mental Health Act 1983 (making circumstance 2 correct and answer D incorrect).

Question 20

Answer **D** — Under s. 18 of the Police and Criminal Evidence Act 1984, a constable may enter and search any premises occupied or controlled by a person who is under arrest for an arrestable offence, if there are reasonable grounds to suspect that there are items on the premises that relate to that offence, *or* to some other arrestable offence which is connected with or similar to that offence. For the purposes of the section, a vehicle is 'premises'. (Therefore, answer B is incorrect).

Under s. 19 of the 1984 Act, an officer may seize anything, which is on premises, if he/she has reasonable grounds for believing that it has been obtained in consequence of the commission of an offence and that it is necessary to do so in order to prevent it from being concealed, lost, damaged, altered or destroyed. Section 19 does not allow the seizure of property for intelligence purposes and answer C is incorrect for this reason.

Where the 'premises' searched is a vehicle (see s. 23), the vehicle can itself be seized (*Cowan v Commissioner of Police for the Metropolis* [2000] 1 WLR 254) (making answer A incorrect).

4   HARASSMENT, HOSTILITY AND ANTI-SOCIAL BEHAVIOUR

STUDY PREPARATION

The focus on community safety within the whole criminal justice process has been sharply defined since the Crime and Disorder Act 1998 and looks set to continue.

As a result, a range of statutory measures have been brought in, giving the police (and other agencies) duties in relation to community safety and powers to help them discharge those duties. Other measures to protect the community from fear, intimidation and anti-social behaviour already existed before the Crime and Disorder Act 1998. Taken together, these measures feature highly in regional and local policing strategies to tackle crime and the fear of crime. This makes them important, not only to police officers but, as a result, to those training and examining police law.

QUESTIONS

Question 1

GULLICK has been found guilty of an offence, which was racially aggravated. The court will shortly impose sentence upon him. With regard to the sentence the court can pass, which of the following statements is correct in relation to taking the aggravating feature into account?

[A]   It must be taken into account, and the court must openly state it did so.
[B]   It can be taken into account, and the court must openly state if it did so.
[C]   It must be taken into account, but the court does not have to state it did so.
[D]   It can be taken into account, but the court does not have to state if it did so.

Question 2

There are several 'old' offences, which were given an aggravating factor by the Crime and Disorder Act 1998 and are now racially aggravated offences. Section 28 of the Act defines racial aggravation and the time during which the hostility must be shown towards the victim. At what time during the commission of the offence should the racial hostility be shown?

[A]   It must be during the offence.
[B]   It can be during the offence or immediately before.
[C]   It can be during the offence or immediately before or immediately after.
[D]   It can be during the offence or immediately before or after doing so.

Question 3

GARNER is a black male, and is visibly a follower of the Rastafarian religion. He is attacked one evening and assaulted. He receives injuries amounting to actual bodily harm (under s. 47 of the Offences Against the Person Act). Police believe that the attack was motivated by GARNER's appearance due to comments overheard during the assault.

Could this offence be classified as racially aggravated?

[A] No, as religious groups can never be racial groups.
[B] No, although some religious groups are racial groups, Rastafarians are not *per se*.
[C] Yes, but only if the hostility was based on GARNER's racial group.
[D] Yes, provided the hostility was based on GARNER being a Rastafarian.

Question 4

GLOVER is a white woman, who is married to a black male. She and her husband are out one afternoon when a group of young black males see them. These males do not believe a white female should be with a black male and begin to use threatening and abusive words and behaviour directed at GLOVER. This is based on her association with her black husband. Their conduct would amount to an offence contrary to s. 4A of the Public Order Act 1986.

Is this offence racially aggravated?

[A] No, because it is not based on GLOVER'S membership of her racial group.
[B] No, because the abuse was not directed towards GLOVER's husband.
[C] Yes, because GLOVER is a member of her husband's racial group.
[D] Yes, because their motive was based on hostility towards a racial group.

Question 5

MEREDITH is a racist. One day he was walking up and down the High Street shouting racial chants. His intention was to stir up racial hatred. The police were called, but MEREDITH spotted the officers and ran off. Two days later the officers see him again. Can the officers arrest MEREDITH for the offence he committed two days earlier (contrary to s. 18 of the Public Order Act 1986)?

[A]   No, there is no longer a power of arrest.
[B]   No, this offence carries no power of arrest.
[C]   Yes, this is an arrestable offence (s. 24 of the Police and Criminal Evidence Act 1984).
[D]   Yes, the statutory power of arrest under the 1986 Act would apply.

Question 6

HEALD is infatuated with his female neighbour, and continually asks her out on a date. She is flattered and not at all threatened by this, but refuses to go out with him. HEALD then starts making indecent phone calls to her in an effort to 'turn her on'. He does not, however, intend his neighbour to be distressed by these calls. She is not threatened and finds it all mildly amusing. Consider the offence outlined in s. 43 of the Telecommunications Act 1984 of improper use of public telecommunications systems.

Has HEALD committed this offence?

[A]   Yes, even although there is no intention to cause distress or such distress caused.
[B]   Yes, just by sending the messages and HEALD could be arrested.
[C]   No, there has to be an intention to cause alarm, harassment or distress.
[D]   No, the receiver of the calls has to be alarmed, harassed or distressed by the calls.

Question 7

TAIT separated from his wife when she became pregnant by another man three months ago. He has instructed a solicitor, VAUX, to represent him at divorce proceedings and has written a letter to VAUX. Part of the letter stated, 'I do not wish to take the child's life after it is born but . . . the Law will take its course after I get rid of it, and I hope prison won't be too bad'.

Which of the following statements is correct?

[A] This would be a threat to kill provided the solicitor feared it would be carried out.
[B] This would be a threat to kill provided TAIT intended that it would be believed.
[C] This would not amount to a threat to kill, as the threat is not immediate or in the immediate future.
[D] This would not amount to a threat to kill, as the threat is merely implied and not direct.

Question 8

BARON has sent two threatening letters to his probation officer. However, the second letter was not received until four and a half months after the first.

Could BARON be guilty of harassment contrary to ss. 1 and 2 of the Protection from Harassment Act 1997?

[A] No, as probation officers are unlikely to be distressed.
[B] No, owing to the length of time between the letters.
[C] Yes, but only if the probation officer is likely to be alarmed and distressed.
[D] Yes, but only if actual distress is caused to the probation officer.

Question 9

STOCKWIN has been stalking a female colleague from work, and on three occasions has caused her to fear that violence will be used against her. On the last two occasions, the woman has run off screaming from STOCKWIN.

In relation to proving an offence under s. 4 of the Protection from Harassment Act 1997, what else, if anything, would need to be proved?

[A] That STOCKWIN actually knew the woman feared violence.
[B] Nothing further, the fact the woman ran away screaming would probably be enough.
[C] That violence was intended by STOCKWIN.
[D] That STOCKWIN was reckless as to whether violence was feared.

Question 10

LOVE has been convicted of an offence of harassment contrary to s. 2 of the Protection from Harassment Act 1997 and has had a restraining order imposed on him (under s. 5 of the Act). Should LOVE breach the order, what should happen to him?

[A] He should be arrested and, where appropriate, charged and bailed.
[B] He should be arrested and taken to court within 24 hours of his arrest.
[C] He should be reported for summons.
[D] He should be reported to the court which imposed the order.

Question 11

The Noise Act 1996 allows for the serving of warning notices in relation to 'excessive noise' emanating from one house which can be heard in another at night.

During what time is 'night'?

[A] 10-30 p.m. – 6-30 a.m.
[B] 10-00 p.m. – 6-00 a.m.
[C] 11-00 p.m. – 7-00 a.m.
[D] 11-30 p.m. – 7-30 a.m.

Question 12

Who can apply for an anti-social behaviour order (ASBO)?

[A] The chief officer of police of the area.
[B] The local authority of the area.
[C] Either the local authority or the chief officer of police of the area.
[D] Both the local authority or the chief officer of police of the area in consultation.

Question 13

An anti-social behaviour order (ASBO) can be passed in respect of a person who has acted in an anti-social manner.

Against whom can that 'anti-social manner' be directed for an ASBO to be relevant?

[A] Any person likely to suffer harassment, alarm or distress from that person.
[B] At least two people likely to suffer harassment, alarm or distress from that person.
[C] Any person, not of the same household, likely to suffer harassment, alarm or distress from that person.
[D] At least two people, not of the same household, likely to suffer harassment, alarm or distress from that person.

Question 14

WATTS was responsible for a house, which was in an extremely poor state and likely to fall down. The house was on a highway that was used by several people including those going to a nearby school. Its ruinous state was endangering people using the highway, and a few have to cross the road every day to avoid it. WATTS has continually refused to do anything about the house.

Could WATTS be guilty of public nuisance?

[A] No, as it does not include omissions, only actions by the accused.
[B] No, as not everyone is affected, only a few had to cross the road.
[C] Yes, provided WATTS intended to cause a public nuisance.
[D] Yes, as the people's material rights have been interfered with.

Question 15

FISHER phones up the local radio station and says 'there's a bomb going off in 10 minutes'; however, no actual location is given. FISHER is doing this as a joke and did not mean the station to take the matter seriously.

Has FISHER committed an offence contrary to s. 51(2) of the Criminal Law Act 1977 (communicating false information)?

[A]   Yes, as the words spoken are sufficient.
[B]   Yes, even though a specific location was not given.
[C]   No, because it was only a practical joke.
[D]   No, as there was no specific location given.

Question 16

Section 85 of the Postal Services Act 2000 deals with sending obscene articles through the post. MARSHALL has sent some indecent pictures, which have accidentally been delivered to a 65-year-old woman, who is a devout Christian.

In deciding if the pictures are 'obscene', what factors will the court take into account?

[A]   The fact that they were sent to an old lady.
[B]   The fact that she found them obscene.
[C]   The fact that a reasonable person may find them obscene.
[D]   The fact that the old lady has Christian views.

ANSWERS

Question 1

Answer **A** — Case law generally dictated that racially aggravated offences should attract a higher penalty. Section 153 of the Powers of Criminal Courts (Sentencing) Act 2000 places this principle on a statutory footing by stating that if an offence was racially aggravated the court must treat that as a factor which increases the seriousness of the offence (answers B and D are therefore incorrect). Section 153 further requires that the court shall state in open court that the offence was so aggravated (answer C is therefore incorrect).

Question 2

Answer **C** — Section 28 of the Crime and Disorder Act 1998 defines the time hostility is shown towards the victim as:

(1) An offence is [racially or religiously aggravated] for the purposes of sections 29 to 32 . . . if (a) at the time of committing the offence, or immediately before or after doing so, the offender demonstrates towards the victim of the offence hostility based on the victim's membership (or presumed membership) of a racial or religious group;

Note the time is not limited to hostility shown during the offence (therefore answer A is incorrect) and is not exclusive to at the time or only before the offence, but does include hostility shown after the offence (therefore answer B is incorrect). However Under s. 28(1)(a) it must be shown that the defendant demonstrated the required hostility:

- at the time of the offence
- immediately before, or
- immediately after committing the offence.

No guidance is given as to how immediately will be interpreted. This will be a matter to be considered by the court in the light of all the circumstances of the case in question.

The hostility must be immediately after however, therefore answer D is incorrect.

Question 3

Answer **D** — Religious groups have now been included into racially aggravated offences as a result of the Anti-terrorism, Crime and Security Act 2001. This means that the former case law (mostly arising in an employment context) over whether religious groups could also be regarded as racial groups is largely irrelevant. The change means that a purely religious group such as Rastafarians (who have been held not to be members of an ethnic group *per se* (*Dawkins* v *Crown Suppliers (Property Services Agency)*, *The Times*, 4 February 1993) are now covered by the aggravated forms of offences therefore answers A and B are incorrect. As the hostility can be based on religious as well as racial groups, answer C is incorrect.

Question 4

Answer **C** — Although s. 28 of the Crime and Disorder Act 1998 states 'the offence is motivated (wholly or partly) by hostility towards members of a racial group' it goes onto to say that it must be 'based on their membership of that group' and not their hostility to that group (which makes D incorrect). This membership obviously would cover the female's husband, but the term membership has been broadened by the Act to include 'association with members of that group' (therefore answer B is incorrect). So although the abuse is not based on her membership of her own racial group, i.e. white, by association she is a member of her husband's racial group, i.e. black (therefore answer A is incorrect).

Question 5

Answer **A** — An offence contrary to s. 18 of the Public Order Act 1986 (using words or behaviour or displaying written material stirring up racial hatred), is not an arrestable offence and therefore answer C is incorrect. However, it does have a statutory power of arrest and therefore answer B is also incorrect). A constable, who need not be in uniform, may arrest without warrant any person whom he reasonably suspects of using threatening etc. words with intent to stir up racial hatred (s. 18(3)) and as this is a 'found committing' power of arrest, answer D is incorrect.

Question 6

Answer **A** — This offence is designed to deal with nuisance calls and the offence is complete when the defendant sends the relevant message or other matter that is, as a matter of fact, indecent, obscene or menacing. There is no need to show intention on the part of the defendant (answer C is therefore incorrect), nor any resultant distress caused (answer D is therefore incorrect). The offence is complete by simply making an indecent phone call. There is, however, no specific power of arrest and in the circumstances s. 25 of the Police and Criminal Evidence Act 1984 is not applicable. Answer B is therefore incorrect. You should note that this offence only applies to a 'public telecommunication system' only and would not include internal, private or workplace telephones.

Question 7

Answer **B** — There are two factors to be proved in the offence of threats to kill contrary to s. 16 of the Offences Against the Person Act 1861 — that the threat was made and that it was made with the intention that the person receiving it would fear that it would be carried out. It does not matter whether the person whose life is threatened so fears or whether the person receiving the threat has such a fear and therefore answer A is incorrect. An implied threat will suffice (see the facts of *R* v *Solanke* [1970] 1 WLR 1) and therefore answer D is incorrect. The threat may be to kill another person at some time in the future and therefore answer C is incorrect. A threat to a pregnant woman in respect of her unborn child is not sufficient if the threat is to kill it before its birth. But if it is a threat to kill the child after its birth, then that would appear to be within the section (*R* v *Tait* [1990] 1 QB 290).

Question 8

Answer **D** — If an accused intends to cause alarm or distress and actually does so, that is likely to meet the requirements of s. 1 (*Baron* v *Crown Prosecution Service* 13 June 2000, unreported), provided he follows a course of conduct. Course of conduct has been considered by the courts. In *Lau* v *DPP* [2000] Crim LR 580, the Divisional Court held that, although only two incidents are necessary, the fewer the number of incidents and the further apart they are, the less likely it is that there will be a finding of harassment. In *Baron*, the court accepted that the more spread out and limited in number the incidents and the more indirect their means of delivery (in this case by letter), the less likely it is that a course of conduct amounting to harassment will be found. However, there is no rule and it will depend upon the facts of each individual case. In *Baron*, two letters sent some four and a half months apart could be a course of conduct amounting to harassment and therefore answer B is incorrect. Note it is alarm *or* distress; the court need only be satisfied that the behaviour involved one or the other (*DPP* v *Ramsdale* [2001] ILR 19 March) and therefore answer C is incorrect. Finally, the court in *Baron* refused to endorse the view that public service employees are less likely to be caused distress by threatening letters and therefore answer A is incorrect.

Question 9

Answer **B** — For an offence of putting people in fear of violence contrary to s. 4 of the Protection from Harassment Act 1997, it has to be shown that that a course of conduct caused a person to fear, on at least two occasions, that violence would be used against them — this is clear from the fact pattern. It must then be shown that the defendant knew or *ought* to have known this and therefore answer A is incorrect. This 'ought to know' can be inferred from previous conversations or conduct (e.g. running away, calling the police, etc.). This is not an offence of 'intent' but is subject to a test of reasonableness against the standard of an ordinary person in possession of the same facts as the defendant and therefore answer C is incorrect. Answer D is incorrect for the same reason. So, knowing the woman had ran away screaming on the last two occasions, is there really anything further the prosecution need to show to prove Stockwin ought to have known that his conduct would cause her to fear violence? Arguably not.

Question 10

Answer **A** — Breach of a restraining order imposed by s. 5 of the Protection from Harassment Act 1997 is an offence in its own right, contrary to s. 5(3) of the Act. It is an 'arrestable offence' and should, where appropriate, be charged and bailed. Unlike some 'family' disputes, the offender does not have to be taken to court within a 24-hour period following arrest and therefore answer B is incorrect. As stated, there is no need to either report the offender to the imposing court or report him for summons to a court and answers C and D are therefore incorrect.

Question 11

Answer **C** — The time as outlined in the Noise Act 1996 is 11 p.m. to 7 a.m. and therefore answers A, B and D are incorrect.

Question 12

Answer **D** — Anti-social behaviour orders (ASBOs) are applied for by the 'relevant authority'. The relevant authority is the local authority *or* the chief officer of police for that local authority area and answers A and B are therefore incorrect. However, the Crime and Disorder Act 1998 is aimed at bringing agencies such as the police and local authorities together. Section 1(2) of the 1998 Act states 'a relevant authority shall not make an application without consulting each other relevant authority', so this effectively imposes dual responsibility and consultation and therefore answer C is incorrect.

Question 13

Answer **C** — For an anti-social behaviour order to be relevant, a person must act in an anti-social manner that caused or was likely to cause harassment, alarm or distress to one or more people not of the same household as himself. So it applies even where only one other person is affected by the 'anti-social manner' and answers B and D are therefore incorrect. The other person should not be from the same household as the person acting in an anti-social manner and answer A is therefore incorrect.

Question 14

Answer **D** — The Court of Appeal has expressed approval of the following definition of public nuisance:

> *A common nuisance is an act not warranted by law or an omission to discharge a legal duty, which act or omission obstructs or causes inconvenience or damage to the public in the exercise of rights common to all of Her Majesty's subjects. (Attorney-General v PYA Quarries Ltd [1957] 2 QB 169).*

This means that public nuisance can be committed by omissions and therefore answer A is incorrect. It is not necessary to prove that every member within a class of people in the community has been affected by the defendant's behaviour; simply that a representative cross-section has been so affected (*PYA Quarries*) and therefore answer B is incorrect. There is no need to prove intent; the *mens rea*, therefore, is that the defendant is guilty of the offence charged 'if either he knew or he ought to have known' that the conduct would bring about a public nuisance (*R v Shorrock* [1994] QB 279). The fact Watts has refused to do anything about the house would be sufficient and answer C is therefore incorrect. The circumstances of this question have been held, in a fairly ancient case, to amount to a public nuisance (*R v Watts* [1757] 1 Salk 357).

Question 15

Answer **C** — A call stating 'there is a bomb' is sufficient to comprise an offence contrary to s. 51(2) of the Criminal Law Act 1977, even though there is no reference to a place or location (*R v Webb, The Times*, 19 June 1995) and answer D is therefore incorrect. So answers A and B could both be correct. However, as this is an offence of 'specific intent' the defendant's intention is a factor. Although it is not necessary for Fisher to have any particular person in mind, the subsection says that the defendant has to have 'the intention of inducing in him or any other person a false belief that a bomb or other thing liable to explode or ignite is present in any place'. It is clear then that Fisher would have to intend that someone believed him and a practical joke would not be covered by this section (answers A and B are therefore incorrect).

Question 16

Answer **C** — Whether an article is obscene is a question of fact for the court to determine in each case. That test will not involve looking at the particular views or frailties of the recipient (answers A, B and D are therefore incorrect) but will be an objective test based on a reasonable bystander (*Kosmos Publications Ltd v DPP* [1975] Crim LR 345).

5 PUBLIC ORDER AND TERRORISM

STUDY PREPARATION

This chapter links two key areas of policing. One is the maintenance of public order using the increasingly wide range of offences and powers that are available to the police; the other is terrorism which, until the introduction of Terrorism Act 2000 and then the events of 11 September 2001, was an area of policing left largely to highly specialist departments.

Between these two areas lies a great deal of law — most of it statutory. In tackling that law it is important to know the elements of the main offences and also the features that distinguish one event from another — including the different powers of arrest.

Changes in the terrorism legislation are clearly very important and highly relevant, particularly the greatly extended definition of terrorism and the additional police powers created by the 2000 Act.

QUESTIONS

Question 1

ANDREWS is out in a town one day with his wife, who is wearing a fur coat, when BROWN an animal rights protestor approached them and says 'You murderer, how many animals have died to clothe you'. BROWN is calm and makes no threat. ANDREWS is infuriated and starts a heated argument. Constable WILLIAMSON is nearby and hears the commotion and goes to investigate. On arrival, ANDREWS tells the officer what had happened and says, 'if this clown isn't taken out of my sight I will not be responsible for my actions'. The officer fears that a breach of the peace will take place and that there will be violence.

Which of the following actions is appropriate or available to the officer?

[A] Arrest ANDREWS for breach of the peace.
[B] Arrest BROWN for breach of the peace.
[C] Arrest neither, as breach of the peace is not taking place currently.
[D] Arrest both for breach of the peace.

Question 2

JENKINS is a heavy drinker, and is well known for being able to handle his liquor. One night he is out drinking with his friends and as a prank one of them drops amphetamine powder into JENKINS's pint of lager. Two hours later, in the street outside the pub, JENKINS begins to shout and swear at people. JENKINS is drunk, having consumed ten pints of lager. Police officers approach him and he shouts and physically threatens the officers. They arrest JENKINS for being drunk and disorderly. At court it is argued that his disorderly behaviour was due entirely to the drug, of which he had no knowledge, and that he is not guilty.

In relation to this offence, which of the following statements is correct?

[A] He may be guilty, as alcohol is a partial cause of his intoxication.
[B] He is guilty, as it is immaterial what caused the intoxication.
[C] He is not guilty, as this offence is not made out where there are several causes of the incapacitated state.
[D] He is not guilty, as the cause of his intoxication was not self-induced.

Question 3

A large crowd has formed outside a national Embassy protesting over that country's perceived intrusive foreign policy. The crowd number 20 people, most of them peaceful, but carrying banners threatening violence against the Embassy staff. About four or five of the protesters are actually shouting threats of violence, and one of the protesters runs from the crowd and attacks the front door of the Embassy.

Given that there is evidence of threats and a common purpose, who, if anyone, is technically guilty of the offence of riot?

[A]   All the crowd are guilty.
[B]   None of the crowd are guilty.
[C]   Only the protestor who attacks the embassy is guilty.
[D]   Those who shout threats of violence are guilty.

Question 4

Whose authority is required before a prosecution for the offence of riot can be brought?

[A]   The Attorney-General.
[B]   The Director of Public Prosecutions.
[C]   The Solicitor-General.
[D]   The Secretary of State.

Question 5

Violence is defined by s. 8 of the Public Order Act 1986. Which of the following statements is correct?

[A]   Violence towards property covers ss. 1, 2 and 3 of the Act.
[B]   It must be violence intended to cause injury.
[C]   It could involve throwing a stone that falls short of its intended target.
[D]   It is violence directed towards a person only.

Question 6

Football supporters, of rival teams, have a large fight after a match. Police begin to arrive and all but three supporters run off. These three continue to fight each other and one is armed with a baseball bat. As a result of the fighting, these three are now the only people in the area, other than the police officers.

Are the three left fighting guilty of 'violent disorder' contrary to s. 2 of the Public Order Act 1986?

[A] Yes, provided a common purpose can be shown.
[B] Yes, all the elements are present.
[C] No, violent disorder is committed by *more* than three people.
[D] No, there was no one present who would fear for his or her safety.

Question 7

Section 12 of the Public Order Act 1986 allows for conditions to be imposed on public processions. THOMAS intends to hold such a procession in four weeks time and the police are considering applying conditions.

How should these conditions be set?

[A] In advance of the day, by the Chief Constable, in writing.
[B] In advance of the day, by the Assistant Chief Constable/Commander, in writing.
[C] On the day, by the senior officer present, in writing.
[D] On the day, by the Chief Constable, orally.

Question 8

Constable JEFFERS, who is in full uniform, has been deployed to deal with a trespassory assembly, in respect of which an order under s. 14A of the Public Order Act 1986 has been obtained prohibiting it taking place. The officer is 4.5 miles from the monument where the assembly was due to take place, and is carrying out powers granted by s. 14C of the 1986 Act, preventing access to the site. The officer has stopped a vehicle, and has directed the occupants not to proceed in the direction of the assembly.

Are the officer's actions lawful?

[A]   Yes, as the officer was in uniform the actions are lawful.
[B]   Yes, the actions are lawful; it is immaterial that the officer was in uniform.
[C]   No, the officer is outside the radius set by the Act at 4 miles.
[D]   No, the officer has no power to stop vehicles under this section.

Question 9

Constable MEREDITH has been called to a public meeting, which is being held in relation to the building of a new trunk road. A person attending the meeting has been acting in a disorderly manner with the purpose of preventing the meeting taking place.

What action can the officer take under s. 1 of the Public Meetings Act 1908 (trying to break up a public meeting)?

[A]   Arrest the offender, using the statutory power.
[B]   Require the offender to leave.
[C]   Require the offender to leave if requested by the chair of the meeting.
[D]   Require the offender's name and address if requested by the chair of the meeting.

Question 10

Section 3 of the Football (Offences) Act 1991 (misbehaviour at designated football match) deals with 'chanting of indecent or racialist nature'. This chanting is defined by s. 3(2)(a).

Which of the following is defined as 'chanting' in relation to the words or sounds uttered?

[A] It must be repeated and in concert with others.
[B] It need not be repeated but must be in concert with others.
[C] It need not be repeated and can be committed acting alone.
[D] It must be repeated and can be committed acting alone.

Question 11

MILLER has organised a trip to a Premier League football match and will be using his seven-seated Multi Passenger Vehicle for transport. At the last minute some of his party drop out and only MILLER and his friend go on the trip. His friend has taken 12 cans of lager on board.

In relation to this taking of intoxicating liquor on board, has there been an offence contrary to s. 1A of the Sporting Events (Control of Alcohol etc.) Act 1985?

[A] No, because of the number of seats on the vehicle.
[B] No, as there are only two people in the vehicle.
[C] Yes, provided MILLER knew intoxicating liquor had been taken on board.
[D] Yes, even though MILLER did not take the intoxicating liquor on board.

Question 12

DAWKINS is entering a designated sports ground and has been searched by a police officer. The officer finds a hip flask on DAWKINS, which contains malt whisky. When questioned, DAWKINS said he had it with him to drink from and did not intend using it to harm anyone.

Has DAWKINS committed an offence contrary to s. 2 of the Sporting Events (Control of Alcohol etc.) Act 1985 (alcohol at sports grounds)?

[A] No, as he has no intention of using the article to cause injury.
[B] No, because the article is not of the kind normally discarded.
[C] Yes, because the article contains intoxicating liquor.
[D] Yes, because the article is capable of causing injury to a person.

Question 13

There is now a generic banning order under the Football (Disorder) Act 2000 dealing with football spectators. In relation to someone who has been convicted of a relevant offence under s. 14A of the Football Spectators Act 1989, e.g. use of violence during a match, what are the court's options in relation to imposing a banning order?

[A] The court should pass such an order, and must state in open court the reasons why such an order was passed.
[B] The court should pass such an order, and must give written notice as to the reasons why such an order was passed.
[C] The court should pass such an order, but must state in open court the reasons for not doing so, if not passed.
[D] The court should pass such an order, but must give written notice as to the reasons for not doing so, if not passed.

Question 14

CHILDS has concocted a white powder made from talcum powder and flour. He has written to several Members of Parliament, as well as some local councillors, threatening that he will post the powder (which he claims to contain the anthrax virus) to them if they do not change their policy on asylum seekers.

Would these threats amount to terrorism as defined by s. 1 of the Terrorism Act 2000?

[A]   Yes, but only if CHILDS was motivated by a political cause.
[B]   Yes, a threat is sufficient to amount to terrorism.
[C]   No, as only a threat has been made at present.
[D]   No, as there was never any actual risk to a person's health or life.

Question 15

GIRVAN is an employee of a well-known High Street Bank. Over the last few months she has been becoming increasingly suspicious of a customer's account and has started to collect information which she suspects demonstrates links between the customer's account and an animal rights group. She suspects, but has no evidence, that the customer is providing money that will be used for acts of terrorism. She has, however, collected information relating to his personal bank account that she suspects to be important.

In relation to disclosing her suspicions to the police, which of the following statements is correct?

[A]   She should disclose the information as soon as it amounts to admissible evidence.
[B]   She must disclose the information now even if it does not amount to admissible evidence.
[C]   She should disclose only her suspicions now, the information she collected is confidential.
[D]   There is no obligation to disclose, it is a matter of choice.

Question 16

PORTER has long been suspected of being involved in money laundering for a proscribed terrorist organisation. He has no previous convictions, nor is there any evidence at all that he is now committing, or that he has in the past committed, any specific offence.

Considering only the power of arrest under s. 41 of the Terrorism Act 2000, could the police arrest PORTER now?

[A] No, as he has no convictions for terrorism offences.
[B] No, as he is not reasonably suspected of committing a specific offence.
[C] Yes, provided he is reasonably suspected of being a terrorist.
[D] Yes, provided he is reasonably suspected of having links to terrorists.

Question 17

In relation to the offence of affray, and the presence of 'a person of reasonable firmness' which of the following statements is true?

[A] There has to be an actual person present who was threatened with violence.
[B] There has to be an actual person present who was in fear for their safety.
[C] There does not have to be anyone present, merely a 'hypothetical person' who may feel threatened with violence.
[D] There does *not* have to be anyone present, as violence conducted towards property is enough.

Question 18

SADIQUE, who is Asian but from Uganda, has bought a product, which has failed to work. He returns it to the shop and is dealt with by AKANJI, a shop assistant who is Nigerian by birth. Less than happy with the service, SADIQUE calls AKANJI 'an African twat' and 'an African bitch'. AKANJI is very distressed by this and contacts the police.

Has SADIQUE committed an offence contrary to s. 31(1)(b) of the Crime and Disorder Act 1998 (racially aggravated intentional harassment, alarm or distress)?

[A]   No, as 'African' does not describe a racial group.
[B]   No, as SADIQUE is from the same racial group as AKANJI.
[C]   Yes, provided SADIQUE intended to distress AKANJI.
[D]   Yes, there is no need to prove intent, provided distress is caused.

ANSWERS

Question 1

Answer **A** — Police officers are expected to focus their attention on those who are likely to present the actual threat of violence or disorder, which was the approach taken by the Divisional Court in the case of *Redmond Bate* v *DPP* [1999] Crim LR 998. The court held that, in this case where preachers who were antagonising passers-by were unlawfully arrested for breach of the peace, the officers should have directed their attention to the passers-by from whom the threat of violence was emanating. The Court of Appeal, in *Bibby* v *Chief Constable of Essex Police, The Times*, 24 April 2000 set out conditions that must be met before the power to arrest for breach of the peace should be used:

- The common-law power to arrest for breach of the peace should be exercised only in the clearest circumstances.
- The threat must come from the person to be arrested.
- His/her conduct must clearly interfere with the rights of others.
- The person to be arrested must be acting unreasonably so as to give rise to a well-founded fear that a breach of the peace will be occasioned.

The second point in the above list makes B and D incorrect as Brown is not making any threats. Also, as the power of arrest can be used to prevent a future breach of the peace, answer C is incorrect. Arresting Andrews would fit the test in *Bibby* and would be lawful. As Brown has made no threat arresting him would be unlawful, as it does not fit the test in *Bibby*.

Question 2

Answer **A** — For this offence the drunkenness must be caused by excessive amounts of alcohol; where this is not the case and his state is caused by some other intoxicant, e.g. a drug, the offence is not made out (*Neale* v *R.M.J.E. (a minor)* (1984) 80 Cr App R 20) and therefore answer B is incorrect. In *Neale*, Goff LJ held that 'drunkenness' means taking intoxicating liquor to an extent that affects steady self-control. However, where there are several causes of a person's intoxicated state, one of which is alcohol, a court can find the person was in fact drunk even though some other intoxicant had an effect on this 'steady self-control' and therefore answer C is incorrect. Answer D is a defence from the Public Order Act 1986 and has no impact on this offence and is incorrect.

Question 3

Answer **C** — Section 1(1) of the Public Order Act 1986 defines riot as:

> Where 12 or more persons who are present together use or threaten unlawful violence for a common purpose and the conduct of them (taken together) is such as would cause a person of reasonable firmness present at the scene to fear for his personal safety . . .

Common purpose may be inferred from the conduct of the rioters together with such circumstances as the carrying of banners, shouting of slogans, threats and the like. However, the most important part of the definition under s. 1(1) is, 'each of the persons using unlawful violence for the common purpose is guilty of riot'. To be guilty, an accused must use, rather than merely threaten, unlawful violence (*R v Jefferson* [1994] 1 All ER 270). So in the question, only the person that uses actual violence is guilty and therefore answers A, B and D are incorrect.

Question 4

Answer **B** — The consent of the Director of Public Prosecutions is required and therefore answers A, C and D are incorrect.

Question 5

Answer **C** — 'Violence' means any violent conduct, so that — except in the context of affray — it includes violent conduct towards property as well as violent conduct towards people. As s. 3 (affray) is not covered, answer A is incorrect. In addition, violence is not restricted to conduct causing or intended to cause injury or damage but includes any other violent conduct (for example, throwing at or towards a person a missile of a kind capable of causing injury which does not hit or falls short) and therefore answers B and D are incorrect.

Question 6

Answer **B** — The definition of violent disorder under s. 2 of the Public Order Act 1986 is 'where 3 or more persons who are present together use or threaten unlawful violence . . . .'. Consequently, three people is enough and answer C is incorrect. The next point to prove is that they were using or threatening violence, which clearly they are, but for this offence you do not have to show a common purpose and therefore answer A is incorrect. Lastly, their conduct must be such that it 'would cause a person of reasonable firmness present at the scene to fear for his personal safety'. However, no such person need be present and the offence is made out where their conduct would cause fear for safety were such a person actually present and therefore answer D is incorrect. The circumstances outlined in the question would amount to a *prima facie* case of violent disorder.

Question 7

Answer **A** — There are two occasions when conditions can be imposed on a procession — in advance or during the procession — and there are differences between them. Where advance notice is given, as in this case, the senior officer designated to carry out the power is the chief officer of police and answers B and C are therefore incorrect. If the conditions are set in advance, they must be in writing and therefore answer D is incorrect. If the procession had began, the power falls to the senior officer present who may make the order orally. However, clearly formal, written notice would probably stave off future litigation.

Question 8

Answer **D** — Under s. 14A of the Public Order Act 1986, the chief officer of police has the power, if he or she reasonably believes that it is intended to hold a trespassory assembly which may result in serious disruption to the life of the community or significant damage to the land, building or monument which is of historical, archaeological or scientific importance, to apply to the district council for an order prohibiting for a specified period the holding of all trespassory assemblies in the district or part of it. The order must not last for more than four days and must not apply to an area greater than that represented by a circle of five miles radius from a specified centre and therefore answer C is incorrect. A constable, who must be in *uniform*, has power to stop someone he reasonably believes to be on his way to an assembly prohibited by an order under s. 14A and to direct him not to proceed in the direction of the assembly and therefore answer B is incorrect. This power, however, does not apply to vehicles and is restricted to 'stop that person' and answer A is therefore incorrect. Other powers exist to stop the vehicle however.

Question 9

Answer **D** — It is an offence, contrary to s. 1(1) of the Public Meeting Act 1908, for a person at a lawful public meeting to act in a disorderly manner for the purpose of preventing the transaction of the business for which the meeting was called. The offence is triable summarily only, and there is no specific power of arrest and therefore answer A is incorrect. There is no power given by this Act to require a person to leave, even at the request of the chair, which makes answers B and C incorrect. However, following a request from the chair, the officer can demand the name and address of the person suspected of committing the offence under s. 1(1). A further offence is committed if the person fails to comply with this demand contrary to s. 1(3) of the 1908 Act.

Question 10

Answer **D** — For the offence under s. 3 of the Football (Offences) Act 1991, the defendant must be shown to have repeated the words or sound before it can be classed as 'chanting' and therefore answers B and C are incorrect. The definition under s. 3(2) has been amended by the Football (Offences and Disorder) Act 1999 to cater for occasions where the offence is committed by one person acting alone and therefore answer A is incorrect for this reason.

Question 11

Answer **A** — This offence is carried out in relation to the type of vehicle, its use and the number of people on board. If it is being used for a journey to or from a designated sporting event, and it is not a public service vehicle but is adapted to carry more than eight passengers, it fits the criteria laid down in s. 1A of the Sporting Events (Control of Alcohol etc. Act 1985). The vehicle in question does not fit the criteria in relation to the number of seats and therefore the offence cannot be committed. As far as the other options are concerned, the number of passengers can be two or more and therefore answer B is incorrect and the offence of carrying intoxicating liquor can only be committed by the driver or owner and therefore answers C and D are incorrect. Having been carried on by the driver, any person in possession of the intoxicating liquor also commits an offence as do those who are drunk on such a vehicle provided the conditions laid down in the statute are met.

Question 12

Answer **C** — An offence under s. 2 of the Sporting Events (Control of Alcohol etc.) Act 1985 is committed by 'a person who has intoxicating liquor or an article to which this section applies in his possession'.

The article to which s. 2 applies is defined as any article capable of causing injury and there is no need to prove intention and therefore answer A is incorrect. However, this article is further defined as:

- bottles, cans or other portable containers (including ones that are crushed or broken), which
- are for holding any drink, and
- are of a kind which, when empty, are normally discarded or returned to, or left to be recovered by, the supplier.

As the hip flask does not fit this definition, answer D is incorrect. The fact that Dawkins is in possession of intoxicating liquor makes him liable; it does not have to be an article to which this section applies. So he commits the offence even though the hip flask is not an article to which s. 2 applies and therefore answer B is incorrect.

Question 13

Answer **C** — Rather than simply having the power to make such banning orders, courts are under a statutory duty to pass such orders where they are satisfied, on reasonable grounds, that such an order is needed to prevent violence at a 'regulated football match'. This is not, however, mandatory, but where such an order is not passed the court must state in open court (and not in writing) why such an order was not passed and therefore answer D is incorrect. Where such an order is passed, the courts are under no statutory obligation to declare why such an order was passed, written or otherwise and therefore answers A and B are incorrect.

Question 14

Answer **B** — Terrorism is now defined by s. 1 of the Terrorism Act 2000 as 'the use or threat of action'. The definition includes a threat so answer C is therefore incorrect. Although the terrorism legislation the 2000 Act replaced was predominantly directed towards the affairs of Northern Ireland, the new Act has been widened. It now recognises that terrorist activity may be motivated by reasons other than simply political ones. As s. 1(1)(c) says, 'the use or threat is made for the purpose of advancing a political, religious or ideological cause' and therefore answer A is incorrect. Although a threat is now sufficient, we have to consider the action that is threatened or used. That action, in relation to people, must involve a risk to their life or a serious risk to their health. Clearly there has been a threat, which if true, would be a risk to peoples' lives and no actual risk needs to be established and therefore answer D is incorrect.

Question 15

Answer **B** — There are a number of offences contained in the Terrorism Act 2000 and some relate to money and its use for the purposes of terrorism. Girvan's suspicions about the customer's activities, if proved to be true, would amount to such an offence. Section 19 of the 2000 Act places a statutory duty on people who form suspicions about activities they believe amount to the offences outlined here, if that belief/suspicion is based on information that comes to their attention in the course of their employment. The duty is to inform the police without delay of those suspicions and answers A and D are therefore incorrect. They must also disclose the information on which it is based and therefore answer C is also incorrect. Failure to comply with this duty is an offence, punishable with five years' imprisonment.

Question 16

Answer **C** — The Terrorism Act 2000 provides officers with an additional power of arrest in relation to 'terrorists'. This complements the existing powers under s. 24 of the Police and Criminal Evidence Act 1984 that exist for most of the offences connected with terrorist activities. It is wide-ranging power in that it does not require reasonable suspicion of involvement in a specific offence and therefore answer B is incorrect. It does not require evidence that the person is now, or has in the past, been a terrorist and, therefore answer A is incorrect. It is sufficient that the officer reasonably suspects the person to be a 'terrorist'. So what is a terrorist? Section 40 of the 2000 Act defines this as a person who:

- has committed an offence under any of sections 11, 12, 15 to 18, 54 and 56 to 63, or
- is or has been concerned in the commission, preparation or instigation of acts of terrorism.

As far as the first statement is concerned, Porter does not fit the definition in the fact pattern. However, where the officer has reasonable grounds to suspect him of being involved in the preparation of acts of terrorism through his money laundering activities, he may be justifiably arrested. This is true even though he is not suspected of a specific terrorist offence. Although it is a broad power, it requires more than mere links to terrorists and answer D is therefore incorrect.

Question 17

Answer **A** — The House of Lords has held that, in order to prove the offence of affray, the threat of unlawful violence has to be towards a person(s) present at the scene (*I and others* v *DPP, The Times,* 9 March 2001). This is violence and not fear for their safety and therefore answer B is incorrect. There does have to be someone present, and in that respect answer D is incorrect. Answer D also incorrect in that violence towards property is specifically *not* included in affray as it is in riot and violent disorder. The second element that needs to be proved relates to the 'hypothetical person present'. It is necessary to prove the defendant's conduct would have caused a hypothetical person present at the scene to fear for his/her personal safety which is more than simply threatened with violence. (*R* v *Sanchez* (1996) 160 JP 321) and therefore answer C is incorrect.

Question 18

Answer **C** — This question loosely follows the circumstances of (*R* v *White (Anthony Delroy)* [2001] 1 WLR 1352, where the Court of Appeal upheld White's conviction for this offence. The Court held that the words used are to be construed as they are generally used in England and Wales and on that basis the word 'African' described a racial group defined by reference to race and therefore answer A is incorrect. The word 'Asians' has been similarly recognised (see *DPP* v *Rishan Kumar Pal* [2000] Crim LR 756). This offence can be committed towards people from the same racial group as the accused and answer B is therefore incorrect. This is a crime of 'specific intent' and as such does require the intent to be proven and therefore answer D is incorrect.

6 FIREARMS

Definitions play a big role in this chapter, and the first few pages are devoted to this area. You must understand these definitions, particularly 'firearm', 'shotgun' and 'imitation firearm' before you move on to the offences. Also, the familiar definitions of 'possession' and 'has with him' appear frequently throughout the legislation and their elements must be known.

There are several offences, involving the criminal use of firearms which you should familiarise yourself with. This can be a confusing area, as some offences appear to cross over. Pay particular attention to those offences that may or may not be committed with an imitation firearm.

Police powers under the Firearms Act 1968 are wide ranging, and some offences carry their own power of entry and search. Do not ignore the various powers under the Act.

Ages play a significant part in this legislation. There is a chart contained in the *General Police Duties Manual* (5.10), which should assist you to learn the several offences relating to ages. Try to learn these.

In tackling questions on firearms, establish exactly what type of weapon is involved. Is it real or imitation? Is it an air weapon?

Note that many firearms offences include the use of air weapons, which usually appear as summary only offences, with no specific powers of arrest.

QUESTIONS

Question 1

BUSH has recently acquired a shotgun, the barrel of which has been shortened, so that it measures only 25 inches.

What authorisation would BUSH require in relation to the weapon?

[A] A firearms certificate to cover his possession.
[B] The permission of the Secretary of State, as it is a prohibited weapon.
[C] A shotgun certificate to cover his possession.
[D] The weapon is now prohibited, and is therefore illegal.

Question 2

NEVILLE has recently acquired a plastic toy gun, which has the appearance of a real pistol. He approaches PARSONS, who owes him money, and uses the gun to threaten him into believing violence will be used unless he repays the debt.

Has NEVILLE committed an offence under s. 16A of the Firearms Act 1968 (possession with intent to cause fear of violence)?

[A] Yes, the offence is complete in these circumstances.
[B] No, this offence may not be committed with an imitation firearm.
[C] No, because the toy cannot be readily converted into a s. 1 firearm.
[D] Yes, provided PARSONS actually believed violence would be used against him.

Question 3

OWEN owned a rifle, for which he had a firearms certificate. He bought another rifle from his friend, VOYLE, whose own licence had expired. OWEN did not have enough room in his own cabinet and asked VOYLE if he could keep the rifle for him until OWEN bought a new cabinet. OWEN intended applying for an extension to his licence when he had the rifle in his home.

Which person, if either, would commit an offence in these circumstances?

[A] Only OWEN, as he has taken possession of the weapon.
[B] Only VOYLE, as OWEN has not yet taken possession of the weapon.
[C] Both people, from the time OWEN bought the rifle.
[D] Only VOYLE, as only one person may be in possession at any one time.

Question 4

Constable CHAVEZ stopped PETERS in his car and when he conducted a PNC check Constable CHAVEZ found that PETERS was wanted for attempted robbery, having threatened a garage cashier with a knife. Constable CHAVEZ searched the car and discovered a firearm in the boot. There was no evidence to show that PETERS was in possession of a firearm at the time of the original offence.

Would PETERS be guilty of an offence contrary to s. 17(2) of the Firearms Act 1968 (possession at time of committing/being arrested for a sch. 1 offence)?

[A] No, he was not in possession of the firearm during the original offence.
[B] Yes, because he has attempted to commit an arrestable offence.
[C] No, because he did not commit the full offence of robbery.
[D] Yes, because he has been arrested for attempting to commit a sch. 1 offence.

Question 5

VEGA was in the Rat and Carrot pub one night, when he sneaked upstairs into the living quarters while the licensee was serving in the bar. He found a loaded air rifle in a bedroom, and carried it with him in case he was disturbed.

Has VEGA committed an offence under s. 20 of the Firearms Act 1968 (trespassing with a firearm)?

[A]   No, he did not enter the building as a trespasser.
[B]   Yes, he has committed the offence in these circumstances.
[C]   No, he was only in possession of an air weapon.
[D]   No, he took possession of the weapon after he became a trespasser.

Question 6

SAUNDERS, a drug dealer, keeps a handgun in his house for protection. One day, he drove to a local shop, where he entered and stole goods. As he was leaving the shop, he was stopped by a store detective. SAUNDERS punched the store detective and ran to his car and escaped. The handgun remained in his house during the incident.

Has SAUNDERS committed an offence under s. 18 of the Firearms Act 1968 (possessing a firearm while committing an indictable offence)?

[A]   No, he did not have the firearm with him at the time of committing the offence.
[B]   No, it cannot be shown that he intended to use the firearm for the commission of the offence.
[C]   Yes, there is no need to show that he intended to use the firearm for the commission of the offence.
[D]   No, as it cannot be shown that he committed an indictable offence.

Question 7

Constable PEARCE attended a noisy house party. As Constable PEARCE arrived, one of the party-goers, BELSHAW, was leaving the party. BELSHAW told Constable PEARCE that he had seen ERNEST, the house owner, with what appeared to be a real pistol. Also, BELSHAW had overheard ERNEST and another male discussing a robbery that was to take place in an all-night petrol station that night.

What powers, if any, would be available to Constable PEARCE under the Firearms Act 1968?

[A] No power under the Act, as ERNEST was not in a public place.
[B] Power to enter the premises without warrant and arrest ERNEST for an offence under the Act.
[C] Power to enter and search the premises without warrant, but only if Constable PEARCE suspects an offence has been committed.
[D] Power to enter the premises without warrant and search for the weapon.

Question 8

Constable MADDOX was on patrol when she saw COLE walking on the pavement, carrying an object wrapped in a blanket under his arm. She established that COLE was 17 years of age and that he was intoxicated. It was revealed that inside the blanket was an air rifle. COLE had pellets for the weapon in his pocket.

Has COLE committed any offences in relation to the air weapon under the Firearms Act 1968 or the Licensing Act 1872?

[A] Yes, he was in possession of a firearm while drunk.
[B] No offence has been committed in these circumstances.
[C] Yes, of possessing a firearm and ammunition in a public place.
[D] Yes, the air rifle should have been in a gun cover.

Question 9

CONNOR owns a large estate and he holds a s. 1 firearms licence for a rifle. His friend, REES, came to stay and asked to go shooting. CONNOR had to go out for the day. However, he gave REES permission to use his rifle on his land, provided he was accompanied by WALTERS, CONNOR's estate manager.

In these circumstances, would REES be exempt from requiring a firearms licence?

[A] No, the holder of the certificate must always be present for the exemption to apply.
[B] Yes, either the holder of the certificate or his servant may be present for the exemption to apply.
[C] No, the holder of the certificate must be on the premises for the exemption to apply.
[D] No, this type of exemption only applies to the holder of a shotgun certificate.

Question 10

DE'SOUZA is 18 years of age and has recently been released from a young offender's institution, having served two years of a three years and six months sentence of detention.

What restrictions, if any, are placed on DE'SOUZA being in possession of a firearm?

[A] He may only possess a firearm after five years from the date of his release.
[B] He may not possess a firearm at anytime from the date of his release.
[C] He may only possess a firearm after three years from the date of his release.
[D] There are no restrictions, as he was not sentenced to a term of imprisonment.

Question 11

In relation to proof required that a person has committed an offence under s. 16 of the Firearms Act 1968 (endangering life), which of the following statements is correct?

It must be proved that:

[A] The person was in possession of a firearm or imitation firearm with intent to endanger the life of another.
[B] The person had with them a firearm or ammunition with intent to endanger the life of another.
[C] The person was in possession of a firearm or ammunition with intent to endanger the life of another.
[D] The person was in possession of a firearm only, with intent to endanger the life of another.

Question 12

PAUL, aged 14, was given an air rifle for his birthday, but he was not allowed to use it unless he was with his brother, DAVID, aged 21. One day, they were in the back garden, with PAUL shooting at tins set up on a wall. Several pellets strayed into their neighbour's garden, but no damage was caused.

Have either PAUL or DAVID committed an offence under the Firearms Act 1968, in these circumstances?

[A] No, neither person has committed an offence in these circumstances.
[B] Yes, by DAVID only, as the person supervising PAUL's use of the weapon.
[C] Yes, by PAUL only, as a person firing pellets beyond the boundary.
[D] Yes, both people have committed an offence in these circumstances.

ANSWERS

Question 1

Answer **C** — A shotgun is a smooth-bore gun with a barrel *not less than 24 inches* in length. Therefore, even though the barrel has been shortened, it is still within the required limit for a shotgun.

A shotgun with a barrel length of *less* than 24 inches will be treated as a s. 1 firearm — requiring a firearm certificate (which is why answer A is incorrect).

There is a list of 'prohibited weapons' under the 1968 Act, and the permission of the Secretary of State is required to possess them. This weapon does not appear on the list, which is why answers B and D are incorrect.

Question 2

Answer **A** — This question tests understanding of two areas: the definition of imitation firearms and s. 16A of the Firearms Act 1968.

There are two types of imitation firearms: 'general imitations' (those which have the appearance of a firearm; and 'imitations of s. 1 firearms' (those which have the appearance of a *s. 1 firearm*, and which can be readily converted into one).

The weapon in the scenario would fall within the first part of the definition, which is why answer C is incorrect.

Under s. 16A of the 1968 Act, a person commits an offence if they have in their possession a firearm *or* imitation firearm, with intent by means thereof to cause any person to believe that unlawful violence would be used against him or another.

Because the offence can be committed with an imitation firearm answer B is incorrect. There is no requirement to prove that the victim actually believed that violence would be used against him, which is why answer D is incorrect.

Question 3

Answer **C** — Under s. 1 of the Firearms Act 1968, it is an offence for a person to have in his possession, or to purchase or acquire a firearm, without holding a certificate in force at the time or otherwise than as authorised by such a certificate.

The Act allows for a person to possess more than one firearm, but they must apply for any new firearm to be included on their certificate.

As Voyle has retained possession of the rifle after his certificate has expired, he clearly commits an offence (which is why answer A is incorrect).

It remains to be proved that Owen is also in possession of the weapon. There is no requirement to prove that he had the weapon *physically* in his possession — possession has a wider meaning than 'has with him'.

It is possible for one person to be in possession, even though some other person has physical control. It is also possible for more than one person to be in possession of the same article, which is why answers B and D are incorrect.

Question 4

Answer **D** — Under s. 17(2) of the Firearms Act 1968, a person is guilty if he is in possession of a firearm, (or imitation), at the time of committing *or* being arrested for *either* committing *or* attempting an offence listed in sch. 1.

There is a list of offences in sch. 1 and these are arrestable offences. However, as not *all* arrestable offences are included in sch. 1 answer B is incorrect.

Answer A is incorrect because the offence may be committed by possessing the firearm while being arrested for a sch. 1 offence regardless of any timescales between the arrest and the original offence (*or* whether the offender even had the firearm with him when that offence was committed).

The offence includes *attempting* to commit a sch. 1 offence and therefore answer C is incorrect.

Question 5

Answer **B** — The offence is committed under s. 20(1) of the Firearms Act 1968 when a person has a firearm or imitation firearm with him and he enters, *or is in* any building *or* part of a building as a trespasser without reasonable excuse.

The offence does not require a person to have entered a building with the weapon — it includes a person who is in a building with one, i.e. takes possession of it when inside (which makes answer D incorrect).

The offence applies in any building *or part* of a building and there is no need to have entered the building as a trespasser (making answer A incorrect).

The offence includes having a firearm or imitation firearm and firearm includes an air weapon (though the offence is summary) and therefore answer C is incorrect.

Question 6

Answer **A** — This offence is similar to s. 17(2) of the Firearms Act 1968 (possession while committing or being arrested for a sch. 1 offence), and the person would probably be guilty of an offence under that section. However, an offence under s. 18 requires a person to *have with him* a firearm at the time of committing an indictable offence. 'Have with him' may include nearby in his car, but would not include in a house as it would not be readily available.

Answer B is incorrect because there is no requirement to show that the person intended to *use* the firearm to commit the offence. (Answer C would be correct if the person had the firearm with him.)

Answer D is incorrect, as 'indictable offence' will include offences which are triable either way.

Question 7

Answer **D** — Two powers are provided under s. 47 of the Firearms Act 1968. First, a constable may require a person in a public place to hand over a firearm for examination (the purpose being to detect offences).

A further power is provided by s. 47 to examine a weapon from a person elsewhere than in a public place — provided the officer has reasonable cause to suspect they are committing or are *about to commit* a relevant offence (offences in s. 18 and s. 20 of the Act apply). Consequently, answers A and C are incorrect.

Answer B is incorrect because the power is provided to enter premises to search for or examine a firearm only — not to arrest (although an arrest is likely to occur if a firearm is found).

Question 8

Answer **B** — The question tests several pieces of legislation. Under s. 19 of the Firearms Act 1968, a person commits an offence if they are in possession of a loaded air weapon or shotgun, or firearm together with suitable ammunition, in a public place. Thus, no offence is committed when a person has an air weapon, together with ammunition and answer C is therefore incorrect.

Section 22(5) makes it an offence for a person *under 17* to carry an air weapon in a public place if it is not securely covered. While it is likely that the blanket would not be viewed as a secure cover, it is irrelevant in these circumstances, as COLE is over 17 (which is why answer D is incorrect).

Lastly, under s. 12 of the Licensing Act 1872, it is an offence to be in possession of *any loaded firearm*, while drunk (no need incidentally to be in a public place). Since the air weapon was not loaded, answer A is incorrect).

Question 9

Answer **B** — There are several exemptions from the requirement to have a firearms certificate. Under s. 16 of the Firearms (Amendment) Act 1988, a person is allowed to borrow a rifle from the occupier of private premises for use on those premises.

It is specified that the borrowing must take place in *either* the occupier's presence or his 'servant's'. There is no specific requirement for the occupier to be on the premises while the 'servant' is with the borrower (making both answers A and C incorrect).

The same exemption applies under s. 11(5) of the Firearms Act 1968 for the holder of a shotgun licence. This is in addition to the exemption provided under the amended Act (which is why answer D is incorrect).

Question 10

Answer **B** — Under s. 21 of the Act, a person who has been sentenced to life imprisonment or three years' imprisonment (which includes detention in a youth offender institution), must not *at any time* have a firearm in their possession.

Note that the restriction applies to a person *sentenced* and therefore it is immaterial that De'Souza did not serve his whole sentence.

Answer A would be correct if De'Souza had been *sentenced* to less than three years' detention, (also covered by s. 21 of the Act). Answer C is merely a false statement and therefore incorrect.

As detention in a young offender institution is included, answer D is incorrect.

Question 11

Answer **C** — The person would have to be in possession of a firearm or ammunition with intent by means thereof to endanger the life of another under s. 16 of the Firearms Act 1968. The offence is also committed when a person is in possession of the same articles with intent that another person would be able to endanger the life of another. As the offence relates to ammunition, as well as a firearm, answer D is incorrect.

Unlike many of the other similar offences, this offence may not be committed with an imitation firearm (making answer A incorrect).

There is no requirement to show that a person had the firearm/ammunition 'with him'. The offence refers to possession, which is a wider requirement (which is why answer B is incorrect).

Question 12

Answer **A** — Under s. 22(4) of the Firearms Act 1968, a person under 14 commits an offence if they have with them an air weapon or ammunition. There is an exception to this rule, when a person is under the supervision of a person over 21, *provided* they are on premises and the missiles are not fired beyond the boundary of the premises.

However, since neither person in the scenario is *under 14*, neither the offence under s. 22(4), or the exception to the offence apply. Therefore neither commits an offence in these circumstances. Both people would have committed the offence had PAUL been under 14 years of age. Consequently, answers B, C and D are incorrect.

7 WEAPONS

STUDY PREPARATION

While the definition contained in s. 1 of the Prevention of Crime Act 1953 appears quite simple, you need to know the component parts to fully understand the offence. Learn the meaning of 'lawful authority', 'reasonable excuse', 'has with him' and 'public place'; there are many decided cases to assist (or confuse) you. You must also, of course, learn the three categories of offensive weapons. Commonly, people tend to confuse the offence under the 1953 Act with the offence of carrying a bladed or sharply pointed article, especially in relation to folding pocket knives and the length of blades. Remember also where the evidential burden lies in relation to proof for both offences, and the special defences under the Criminal Justice Act 1988.

One of the greatest problems in this very relevant area is separating the different statutory requirements. It is essential to· be able to distinguish between the requirements relating to offensive weapons (in the Prevention of Crime Act 1953) and those relating to pointed or bladed instruments as regulated by the Criminal Justice Act 1988. Unless you are very clear about these differences, life will get very confusing.

Further offences contained in the chapter relate to the carrying of weapons on educational premises. These mirror the two offences above, with similar definitions. Also, you must be able to tell the difference between an 'offensive weapon' and a 'weapon of offence', as contained in the offence of trespassing with a weapon of offence, under the Criminal Law Act 1977. The manufacture and sale of weapons receive attention, with a long list of weapons that may not be manufactured or sold etc. Further offences may be committed by selling and marketing knives and articles to children under 16. Do not forget to learn about crossbows and the three offences contained in the Crossbows Act 1987. Also, pay attention to the powers given to a constable to search people and vehicles.

Apart from that, it is very straightforward!

QUESTIONS

Question 1

Constable RICHARDS stopped POWER and conducted a search under s. 1 of the Police and Criminal Evidence Act 1984. The officer discovered a flick knife in POWER's trouser pocket. POWER stated that he had a reasonable excuse for the weapon being there.

In relation to POWER's claim to have a reasonable excuse, where does the burden of proof lie?

[A] The prosecution must show on the balance of probabilities that POWER did not have a reasonable excuse.

[B] POWER must show beyond reasonable doubt that he did have a reasonable excuse.

[C] The prosecution must show beyond reasonable doubt that POWER did not have a reasonable excuse.

[D] POWER must show on the balance of probabilities that he had a reasonable excuse.

Question 2

In which of the following circumstances may a person claim a reasonable excuse to a charge of having an offensive weapon with them?

[A] Carrying a knife at a football match, in case they are attacked.

[B] Carrying a flick knife in the glove compartment of a car, having forgotten to remove it the day before.

[C] Attending a party carrying a truncheon, as part of a fancy dress costume.

[D] Carrying a flick knife, but not being aware that it is an offensive weapon.

Question 3

MARTIN is a security guard in a night club and, when he is working, he carries a truncheon underneath his jacket. The club has a violent reputation and he carries it to protect himself, as he has been assaulted in the past. The club is open to any paying member of the public, and MARTIN only carries the truncheon inside the premises.

Does MARTIN commit any offences under the Prevention of Crime Act 1953?

[A] No, because the public have to pay to enter the club.
[B] Yes, because he is in a place to which the public has access.
[C] No, because he is not in a public place.
[D] Yes, because he is not at his place of abode.

Question 4

FAWCETT was driving home from work, when he caused another car, being driven by GRANT to brake sharply. GRANT followed him, shouting obscenities and sounding his horn. When FAWCETT stopped at traffic lights, GRANT got out of his car and ran towards him. FAWCETT got out of his own car and picked up a steering wheel lock, and threw it at GRANT, intending to injure him.

Is the steering wheel lock an 'offensive weapon' in these circumstances?

[A] No, FAWCETT formed the intention to use the article after it came into his possession.
[B] Yes, as soon as FAWCETT formed the intention to use the article.
[C] Yes, because FAWCETT used the article, intending to injure GRANT.
[D] Yes, as soon as FAWCETT picked the article up, with the intention to use it.

Question 5

Constable BAKER was on patrol when she stopped a vehicle owned and being driven by CLEMENT. In the front passenger seat was HARVEY. Constable BAKER made a search of the vehicle and discovered a flick knife in the glove compartment.

Could HARVEY and CLEMENT be guilty of an offence under the Prevention of Crime Act 1953?

[A]   No, only CLEMENT may commit the offence, being the owner of the car.
[B]   Yes, the offence is complete against both; no further proof is required.
[C]   No, it is not possible for two people to have the same weapon with them.
[D]   Yes, provided they both knew that the other person had it with him at the time.

Question 6

PENFOLD was stopped and searched on his way to a football match while he was walking in High Street. The searching officer, Constable MARRIOTT, discovered in PENFOLD'S pocket a number of 50 pence pieces that had been sharpened around the edges. Believing that they were offensive weapons, the officer arrested PENFOLD.

In order to prove that PENFOLD was guilty of possessing an offensive weapon would Constable MARRIOTT need to prove intent by PENFOLD to use the coins to cause injury?

[A]   No, provided it can be shown that the coins have been made to cause injury.
[B]   Yes, because there is no apparent victim in these circumstances.
[C]   Yes, because the coins are not offensive weapons *per se*.
[D]   No, provided it can be shown the coins have been adapted to cause injury.

Question 7

BARRY was stopped and searched in the street by Constable ROCH. The officer found a pocket-knife in BARRY'S pocket, which had a four-inch blade. BARRY admitted that he was on his way to a football match and intended to use the knife in a fight with rival fans.

Would Constable ROCH have a power of arrest in these circumstances?

[A]   Yes, as the blade is more than three inches long it is an offensive weapon.
[B]   Yes, a folding pocket-knife with a blade of more than three inches will always be an offensive weapon.
[C]   Yes, it is an offensive weapon regardless of the length of the blade.
[D]   No, a folding pocket-knife will not be an offensive weapon regardless of the length of the blade.

Question 8

DAWSON was stopped and searched in a public place whilst carrying a screwdriver. The end of the screwdriver had been sharpened to a point.

Would DAWSON commit an offence under the Criminal Justice Act 1988 in these circumstances?

[A]   Yes, the screwdriver would be covered by this section, provided it was more than three inches in length.
[B]   Yes, the screwdriver is covered in these circumstances alone.
[C]   No, a screwdriver will not be covered by this section, as it does not have a blade.
[D]   Yes, but the screwdriver would only be covered by this section if DAWSON intended using it to cause injury.

Question 9

The Criminal Justice Act 1988 makes provision for a 'good reason' for carrying a weapon in a public place. In which, if any, of the following situations could a person claim 'good reason' under the Act?

1. A person carries a dagger as part of a national costume.
2. A person carries a dagger as part of a fancy dress costume.
3. A joiner carries a knife on his way to work.

[A] All three situations.
[B] Situations 1 and 3 only.
[C] Situations 2 and 3 only.
[D] None of the above situations.

Question 10

HUTCHINGS visited his friend, CARTER, who lives with his parents in the caretaker's house of a primary school. When he arrived, both boys played in the garden of the caretaker's house. Both boys were playing with flick knives.

Who would commit an offence of having with him an offensive weapon on educational premises in these circumstances?

[A] Neither, because they are not on educational premises.
[B] Both, because they are on educational premises.
[C] HUTCHINGS only, because he does not reside on the premises.
[D] Both, because they are not in a dwelling on educational premises.

Question 11

A report was received by the police of a disturbance in a high school. The first person to arrive was Constable SANCHEZ, who was in plain clothes. He was told that two pupils had threatened a teacher and that one of them had a knife. After a search, Constable SANCHEZ found the two youths in the street outside.

What powers would Constable SANCHEZ have under the Criminal Justice Act 1988 in these circumstances?

[A] He has no powers under the 1988 Act and must use his powers under the Police and Criminal Evidence Act 1984.
[B] He has a power under the 1988 Act to search the youths for an offensive weapon.
[C] He has no powers under the 1988 Act as the pupils were not trespassing.
[D] He has no powers under the 1988 Act as he is not in uniform.

Question 12

Constable SNELL attended a disturbance at a premises belonging to FRASER. FRASER stated that TAYLOR, who was a tenant renting the house, had refused to leave having been served with an eviction notice. TAYLOR was in the detached garage and had armed himself with a baseball bat and was threatening to use it on anyone who tried to make him leave.

Has TAYLOR committed an offence under the Criminal Law Act 1977 in these circumstances?

[A] Yes, he was trespassing with a weapon of offence.
[B] No, because he was not in a dwelling as a trespasser.
[C] No, because he was not in a building attached to a dwelling as a trespasser.
[D] No, because he did not enter the premises as a trespasser.

Question 13

ANDREWS owned a house which was being renovated. One day he visited it and found HARVEY squatting inside. ANDREWS asked HARVEY to leave. However, HARVEY was carrying a knife and threatened ANDREWS with it. ANDREWS went outside to call the police but by the time Constable RAMAN arrived, HARVEY had left and was walking down the road.

What powers would be available to Constable RAMAN to arrest HARVEY for trespassing with a weapon of offence under s. 8 of the Criminal Law Act 1977?

[A] A power of arrest provided he is in uniform.
[B] No powers of arrest as HARVEY is no longer committing the offence.
[C] There is no power of arrest for this offence.
[D] A power of arrest whether he is in uniform or not.

Question 14

STONE owns a shop which sells second-hand goods and has a reputation for being able to supply unusual weapons. COLLINS entered the shop looking for some weapons for himself and his friends for a football match the following week. STONE indicated that he could get his hands on some knuckledusters, which he could sell at a good price. COLLINS agreed to return three days later to buy them.

At what point, if any, would STONE commit an offence under the Criminal Justice Act 1988?

[A] Not until he actually sells the weapons to COLLINS.
[B] Not until he is in possession of the weapons with intent to sell them.
[C] When he offered to sell them to COLLINS.
[D] Not until he has the weapons with him with intent to sell them.

Question 15

WENDY, aged 15, has a Saturday job, working in a chemist's shop owned by HUSSEIN. One day she served PETER, who bought a packet of cartridge razor blades. WENDY was aware that PETER was also 15 as she was in his class at school.

Would either WENDY or HUSSEIN commit an offence of selling a bladed instrument to a person under 16 under s. 141A of the Criminal Justice Act 1988?

[A]   Neither, the articles are not covered by the Criminal Justice Act 1988.
[B]   Both WENDY and HUSSEIN.
[C]   Neither, as WENDY was also under 16.
[D]   WENDY only as HUSSEIN would have a statutory defence.

Question 16

GUY, aged 15, was in the back garden of his parents' house, and had with him a crossbow. He was using it to fire at a target in the garden, and was accompanied at the time by PREECE, aged 18. At no time did any of the bolts fired from the crossbow leave the garden.

Has GUY committed an offence in these circumstances?

[A]   No, because he was accompanied by a person over 18.
[B]   No, because he was not in a public place.
[C]   No, because none of the missiles were allowed to leave the property.
[D]   Yes, because he was not accompanied by a person over 21.

Question 17

Which of the following statements, if either, is/are correct in relation to a police officer exercising their power of search under the Crossbows Act 1987?

1. They must be in uniform to exercise a power of search under the Act.
2. They may enter any land, other than a dwelling house, in order to conduct the search.

[A] Statement 1 only.
[B] Statement 2 only.
[C] Both statements.
[D] Neither statement.

ANSWERS

Question 1

Answer **D** — The prosecution must first show, beyond reasonable doubt, that the defendant had an offensive weapon with him — which in these circumstances should cause no problem. The burden of proof then lies with the defendant to show that he had lawful authority for having the weapon and therefore answers A and C are incorrect. The burden of proof will be judged on the balance of probabilities, *not* beyond reasonable doubt and therefore answer B is incorrect.

Question 2

Answer **C** — There are occasions where a person may have a reasonable excuse for having an offensive weapon with them. In *Houghton* v *Chief Constable of Greater Manchester Police* (1986) 84 Cr App R 319, it was held that where a defendant was in a fancy dress costume as a police officer and carrying a truncheon, the person had a reasonable excuse for having it with them.

It is *not* a reasonable excuse to have a weapon with you as a general precaution against being attacked (*Evans* v *Hughes* [1972] 1 WLR 1452) and answer A is therefore incorrect.

Not being aware you have an offensive weapon with you (*R* v *Densu* [1998] 1 Cr App R 400) or forgetting that you have one in the car when driving (*R* v *McCalla* (1988) Cr App 372) are *not* reasonable excuses and therefore answer B is incorrect. Also, a person must know that they have an article in their possession, even if they have forgotten (*McCalla*). In *Densu*, the defence claimed that although the defendant knew that he had the article with him, he did not know it was an offensive weapon. This was held not to be a reasonable excuse and therefore answer D is incorrect.

Question 3

Answer **B** — The offence may only be committed in a public place, which includes any highway *and* any other premises or place to which at the material time the public are, or are permitted, to have access, whether on payment or otherwise (s. 1(4) of the Prevention of Crime Act 1953) and therefore answers A and C are incorrect.

In order to show that a place is a 'public place', it needs to be shown that those people who are admitted are members of the public and are not admitted as members of some particular class of the public (i.e. belonging to some club), or as a result of some characteristic not shared by the general public at large. In the case of *Paterson* v *Ogilvey* 1957 SLT 354, a field used in an agricultural show was deemed to be a public place. The fact that people were asked to pay to enter is of no consequence, provided *any* member of the public was allowed to pay. It is immaterial for this offence whether you are at your place of abode or not and therefore answer D is incorrect.

Question 4

Answer **A** — The expression, 'has with him', will not in most cases include circumstances where a person has an 'innocent' article, which he or she uses offensively. The purpose of the Prevention of Crime Act 1953 is to prevent people from arming themselves for some future event, and the intention of the Act is to deal with preventative issues.

The case of *Ohlson* v *Hylton* [1975] 1 WLR 724 demonstrates this. The defendant had a bag of tools with him in the course of his trade. He produced a hammer from the bag and used it to hit someone. The court held that, as he had formed the intention to use the hammer *after* it came into his possession, the offence was not made out (answers B and C are therefore incorrect). This decision was followed by several other similar cases (*Bates* v *Bulman* [1979] 1 WLR 1190, *R* v *Dayle* [1974] 1 WLR 181 and *R* v *Humphreys* [1977] Crim LR 225).

This is not to say that 'innocent' articles may never become offensive weapons, such as people carrying screwdrivers to defend themselves, it depends on the immediacy of the conversion from one to another and therefore answer D is incorrect.

Question 5

Answer **D** — It is possible for more than one person to have the same weapon 'with them', (*R* v *Edmonds* [1963] 2 QB 142) and therefore answers A and C are incorrect. It would be necessary to prove that they knew of the existence of the weapon in the hands of the other.

In this case it was decided that both parties knew of the existence of the weapon and that they knew the other party had it 'with him' at the time of the offence. Answer B is incorrect as the offence is not complete until this is proved.

Question 6

Answer **D** — The prosecution would have to show that the coins have been adapted to cause injury in order to show that they are offensive weapons. However, once the prosecution have proved this, there is no need to show an intention to use them to cause injury (*Davis* v *Alexander* (1970) Cr App R 398).

Answer A is incorrect because the coins have not been 'made' to cause injury; they are not offensive weapons *per se*. However, the fact that they are not offensive weapons *per se* still does not place a burden upon the prosecution to prove intent to use them (*Davis* v *Alexander*), which is why answer C is incorrect.

Answer B is incorrect because it is the adaptation of the article that is relevant, not the intention of the person carrying it (*Bryan* v *Mott* (1975) 62 Cr App R 71).

If Penfold were charged under the third leg of the definition, where the weapon is *intended* to cause injury, the prosecution would have to prove an intention to cause injury by Penfold. This would obviously be a harder case to prove than *adaptation* in the above circumstances.

Question 7

Answer **C** — Under the Prevention of Crime Act 1953, an offensive weapon is an article, which is made, intended or adapted for causing injury. The weapon in question will be an offensive weapon, because Barry intends that it will be used to cause injury.

Under the 1953 Act, it is irrelevant what length the blade happens to be. However, under s. 139 of the Criminal Justice Act 1988, a person commits an offence if they have a bladed or sharply pointed instrument in a public place — *unless* the instrument is a folding pocket knife with a blade less than three inches. *Do not mix the two Acts.*

Answers A and B are incorrect as they refer to the length of the blade as being relevant. Answer D is incorrect because a folding pocket-knife may be an offensive weapon, depending on the circumstances.

Question 8

Answer **B** — Under s. 139 of the Criminal Justice Act 1988, a person commits an offence if they have a bladed *or* sharply pointed instrument in a public place. As the Act provides for either a sharp point or a blade answer C is incorrect. It was held in *R v Davies* [1998] Crim LR 564 that a screwdriver will not ordinarily be a bladed instrument, as it does not have a blade. However, this docs not prevent it becoming a sharply pointed instrument, depending on the circumstances.

Under the Act, a folding pocket-knife is excluded, provided the cutting edge of the blade is less than three inches long. This does not apply to all instruments, which is why answer A is incorrect.

There is no requirement under the Act to prove an intention to use the instrument to cause injury and therefore answer D is incorrect.

The screwdriver would obviously fall under the definition of an offensive weapon that was adapted to cause injury. However, note that the question asked for offences under the Criminal Justice Act 1988 only.

Question 9

Answer **B** — Section 139 of the Criminal Justice Act 1988 provides that a defendant may show that he or she has 'good reason' or 'reasonable excuse' for having with them a sharply pointed or bladed article in a public place.

The Act also provides three circumstances where a person may have such an instrument: for use at work (e.g. carpenters, joiners); for religious reasons (e.g. a Sikh carrying a *kirpan*); or as part of a national costume (e.g. someone in Highland dress carrying a *skean dhu*). Therefore statements 1 and 3 are correct.

Carrying such an article as part of a fancy dress costume would not be specifically covered under the Act, which is why statement 2 is incorrect. Consequently, answers A, C and D are incorrect.

Question 10

Answer **A** — This offence was added to the Prevention of Crime Act 1953, and a further offence was added to the Criminal Justice Act

1988 of having a sharply pointed or bladed instrument on school premises. The definitions of weapons mirror the original offences; therefore, it follows that a flick knife will be an offensive weapon *per se*.

Under the definition of 'school premises', the offence may only be committed on premises providing primary or secondary education, or both, whether full-time or part-time.

The offence will *not* be committed on *land occupied solely as a dwelling by a person employed at the school.* This means a caretaker's house in a school. Answer B is incorrect for this reason.

The fact that one of the people was not a resident is not relevant (which is why answer C is incorrect), and the exemption applies to both the land and the dwelling (therefore answer D is also incorrect).

Question 11

Answer **A** — Under the Criminal Justice Act 1988, an offence is committed when a person has an offensive weapon with him on school premises.

Under the Act, a constable may enter school premises and search those premises and any person for an offensive weapon. Note that the power under the Act only enables a constable to enter and search premises and search people *on the premises.* The power is not extended to searching people *off school premises.* The officer may, of course, use his power under s. 1 of the Police and Criminal Evidence Act 1984 to search the youths. This is why answer A is correct and answer B is incorrect.

There is no requirement for the constable to be in uniform and therefore answer D is incorrect.

A person may commit an offence under this Act whether they are on the premises lawfully or not and therefore answer C is incorrect.

Question 12

Answer **D** — Under s. 8 of the Criminal Law Act 1977, a person commits an offence when they are on premises as a trespasser, *having entered as one,* if without lawful authority or reasonable excuse they have with them a weapon of offence.

The baseball bat may well have been a weapon of offence, because of Taylor's intention to use it as such. However, the offence may only be committed where a person has *entered as a trespasser*. Taylor had obviously not done so as he was a bona fide tenant when he entered, which makes answer D correct and answer A incorrect.

Answers B and C are incorrect statements because premises includes, amongst other things, any building and the site comprising any buildings with ancillary land. The offence is *not* restricted to a dwelling house.

Question 13

Answer **B** — A constable *in uniform* may arrest a person who is (or who is suspected to be) *committing* the offence.

Answer A would be correct if Harvey was still committing the offence when the officer arrived — but only if the officer was in uniform (which is why answer D is incorrect).

Answer C is incorrect because there is a power of arrest as can be seen above.

Question 14

Answer **C** — Section 141 of the Criminal Justice Act 1988 makes it an offence to manufacture, sell, hire, *offer* for sale or hire, expose, have in possession for the purpose of sale or hire or lend or give to another person, any weapon listed in the schedule to the Act (knuckledusters are included).

The offence may be committed by making an offer — the Act makes no mention of being in possession of the article when the offer is made, which is why answer C is correct. (This is similar to a case of offering to supply drugs under the Misuse of Drugs Act 1971).

Although offences would be made out in answers A and B the offence has already been committed.

Answer D would be an incorrect answer in any circumstances, as unlike the original 1953 Act, which requires a person to have the weapon with them, this offence deals with possession for the purpose of sale or hire.

Question 15

Answer **A** — Under s. 141A of the Criminal Justice Act 1988 it is an offence for *any person* to sell to a person under 16 a knife, blade, razor blade, axe, any article which has a blade or sharp point *and* is made or adapted for causing injury. The offence *does not* apply to a razor blade in a cartridge, where not more than 2 mm of the blade is exposed (or a folding pocket knife with a blade of less than 3 inches).

The age of the person making the sale is not relevant (which is why answer C is incorrect). There is a defence provided for the person charged to show that they took all reasonable precautions and exercised due diligence to avoid the offence. However, since no offence took place, it is not relevant in these circumstances. If it were relevant, it would only be available to the person making the sale, as the offence only applies to that person (therefore answers B and D are incorrect). It would not apply to Wendy, as she was aware of Peter's age.

Question 16

Answer **D** — Under s. 3 of the Crossbows Act 1987, a person who has with him a crossbow (or parts of a crossbow), capable of discharging a missile is guilty of an offence, unless accompanied by a person who is over 21 (which makes answer A incorrect).

There is no requirement for the person to be in public place and therefore answer B is incorrect. Answer C is incorrect as the statement is taken from the Firearms Act 1968, in relation to air weapons.

Question 17

Answer **B** — If a *constable* (no mention of uniform), reasonably suspects a person is or has committed an offence under s. 3 of the Crossbows Act 1987, he or she may search the suspected person or their vehicle for the crossbow (or parts).

For the purposes of exercising the power of search, a constable may enter any land *other than a dwelling house*, in order to conduct the search.

As only statement 2 is correct, answers A, C and D are incorrect.

8 CIVIL DISPUTES

STUDY PREPARATION

After the wealth of detail covered by the previous few chapters, this one may come as something of a relief.

Although the title would tend to suggest that the police have little interest or involvement, civil disputes are never the less a significant feature of police patrol work. Domestic disputes in particular have attracted considerable attention from ACPO and the Home Office over recent years.

In addition to the various statutory measures in place to govern civil dispute, it is in this area that some of the most difficult 'balancing acts' in relation to human rights issues takes place. These issues should be borne in mind when addressing questions in this chapter.

QUESTIONS

Question 1

Employees of a company are currently on strike; however a few have remained at work. One employee, HIGGINS, who is still working, is followed home by two of the 'strikers'; they call him a 'scab' and a 'strike breaker'. They also whistle and jeer him. HIGGINS is very distressed by this behaviour. Consider the offence of intimidation or annoyance by violence or otherwise contrary to s. 241 of the Trade Union and Labour Relations (Consolidation) Act 1992.

Has this offence been committed?

[A] No, because there needs to be more than two people following HIGGINS.

[B] No, because they are not threatening or intimidating HIGGINS or using violence.

[C] Yes, provided the strikers intended to compel HIGGINS to join the strike.

[D] Yes, provided the strikers intended to cause the distress that HIGGINS suffered.

Question 2

ASHTON has been sacked from his job at an aeronautical factory. He complains to his union, who take four weeks to decide his case. The union eventually decides to authorise industrial action and to picket the aeronautical factory. In the intervening period, however, the firm has moved premises and no longer occupies the premises where ASHTON worked. A considerable amount of land at the new factory is private.

In relation to picketing which of the following is true?

[A] The pickets cannot enter onto the private land to picket.

[B] The pickets could picket the new premises as it is still technically ASHTON'S place of work.

[C] There would be a maximum of six pickets allowed at any one time.

[D] The right to picket outside the factory is an absolute right and cannot be overridden.

Question 3

DAWKINS has had a non-molestation order taken out against him by his wife, which has a power of arrest attached. DAWKINS breaches the order and is arrested at 10.30 pm on Saturday night. He arrives at the police station at 10.35 pm and detention is authorised at 10.55pm.

By what time must DAWKINS be brought before the relevant judicial authority?

[A] Sunday no later than 10.30 pm.
[B] Sunday no later than 10.35 pm.
[C] Monday no later than 10.30 pm.
[D] Monday no later than 10.35 pm.

Question 4

MUSGRAVE is 15 years old and under the care of social services following an abusive home life. She wishes to take out a non-molestation order to prevent her uncle from contacting her, as he regularly approaches her to tell her that her father is sorry.

Under the Family Law Act 1996, can MUSGRAVE apply for a non-molestation order?

[A] No, as a non-molestation order only applies to spouses or former partners.
[B] No, as a person under 16 cannot apply for a non-molestation order.
[C] Yes, provided social services are satisfied she has sufficient understanding to make the application.
[D] Yes, provided the court is satisfied she has sufficient understanding to make the application.

Question 5

Section 16 of the Domestic Proceedings and Magistrates' Courts Act 1978 allows for an applicant to apply to the courts for an order preventing the respondent from using, or threatening to use violence against the applicant. Should such an order be imposed, the court may attach a power of arrest to it.

In what circumstances can a power of arrest be attached to the order?

[A] If the respondent has previously threatened violence to the applicant.
[B] If the respondent has previously physically injured the applicant and the court considers it likely again in the future.
[C] If the respondent has previously physically injured the applicant.
[D] If the respondent has previously threatened violence to the applicant and the court considers it likely again in the future.

ANSWERS

Question 1

Answer **C** — This is an offence of 'specific intent' and as such there has to be an element of intention to bring about a specific outcome. It is committed by 'two or more persons' (therefore answer A is incorrect), where they follow the victim 'in a disorderly manner in or through any street or road'. There does not have to be a threat or use of violence; disorder would be sufficient and therefore answer B is incorrect. Their intention must be to compel Higgins to join the strike, and not simply to cause distress and therefore answer D is incorrect. (Note that if the circumstances were reversed and Higgins was on strike, the offence would still be committed by compelling him to *return* to work.)

Question 2

Answer **A** — Although picketing is lawful under s. 220 of the Trade Union and Labour Relations (Consolidation) Act 1992, there are some restrictions. It is lawful to picket your former place of work if the action is as a result of the termination of your employment. However, a person's place of work does not include new premises of an employer who has moved since dismissing the people picketing (*News Group Newspapers Ltd* v *SOGAT'82 (No. 2)* [1987] ICR 181) and therefore answer B is incorrect. The 1992 Act does not place restrictions on the number of pickets; the number six is from the agreed Code of Practice on picketing which has no legal force and therefore answer C is incorrect. Note, however, that if numbers are large enough, there might be a presumption that the pickets intend to intimidate others, which would make it unlawful (*Broome* v *DPP* [1974] AC 587). If there is a real danger of any offence, (e.g. public disorder) being committed, the pickets have no right to attend at the factory to picket under s. 220 (*Piddlington* v *Bates* [1960] 3 All ER 660) and therefore answer D is incorrect. Section 220 does not authorise pickets to enter onto private land (*British Airports Authority* v *Ashton* [1983] 1 WLR 1079).

Question 3

Answer **C** — If a power of arrest is attached to a non-molestation order under s. 47 of the Family Law Act 1996 and the respondent is arrested for breaching that order, he must be brought before the relevant judicial authority within the period of 24 hours beginning at the time of his arrest. In reckoning for the purposes of s. 47 any period of 24 hours, no account is to be taken of Christmas Day, Good Friday, or any Sunday (s. 47(7)) and therefore answers A and B are incorrect. Note that it is 24 hours from the time of the arrest and not from the 'relevant' time therefore answer D is incorrect.

Question 4

Answer **D** — A non-molestation order under the Family Law Act 1996 does not only apply to spouses or former partners; it applies to anyone who is 'associated' with the respondent (s. 62). This association applies to relatives (s. 62(3)(d)) and therefore answer A is incorrect.

A child under the age of 16 may not apply for a non-molestation order except with the leave of the court (s. 43(1)) and therefore answer B is incorrect. The court may grant leave for the purposes of subsection (1) only if it is satisfied that the child has sufficient understanding to make the proposed application for the order. Note that it is the opinion of the court not social services which counts and therefore answer C is incorrect.

Question 5

Answer **D** — Section 18 of the Domestic Proceedings and Magistrates' Courts Act 1978 deals with the attachment of a power of arrest. Even though s. 16 deals with use or threats of violence, it is only where the court is satisfied that the respondent physically injured the applicant that an order is imposed and therefore answers A and B are incorrect. Also, the court must be satisfied that the respondent is likely to physically injure the respondent again in the future and therefore answer C is incorrect.

9 ANIMALS

STUDY PREPARATION

As a subject area, animals is pretty wide. Encompassing criminal offences, powers of arrest, search and seizure this subject area deals with legislation designed both to protect animals from people and vice versa — all of which can differ depending on the type of animal involved.

A good starting point is to divide the subject into dogs on the one hand and everything else on the other. As well as enjoying the general protection accorded to other domestic mammals, dogs also have a fair amount of legislation of their own.

Although we have come a long way since the days of police exam questions where exotic goldfish got bitten by grass snakes at the village fetes, there is still some important and relevant legislation to be found in this chapter.

QUESTIONS

Question 1

CURSON, aged 16, owns a Doberman, which was given to him on his birthday by his father. One day, his dog escaped from his garden and entered his neighbour's garden, where it attacked and bit a 7-year-old child on the arm.

Who, if either (CURSON or his father), would be liable under the Dangerous Dogs Act 1991, in these circumstances?

[A] Neither, as the dog was not in a public place.
[B] Both, but CURSON's father would have a statutory defence.
[C] Only CURSON as the owner of the dog.
[D] Both, and neither would have a statutory defence.

Question 2

HALL is the owner of a pit bull terrier, which is 12 years old. He took it out in his car one day, and was accompanied by his daughter MELANIE, aged 17. HALL stopped in the street to go into the bank, and left the dog in the car with MELANIE. He was gone for 15 minutes, during which time, Constable WATTS passed by and recognised the breed of dog in the car. The dog had a muzzle, but was not on a lead.

Has HALL committed an offence under s. 1 of the Dangerous Dogs Act 1991 in these circumstances?

[A] No, as the dog was not in a public place.
[B] Yes, an offence was committed in these circumstances.
[C] No, as the dog was wearing a muzzle.
[D] No, as MELANIE was over 16.

Question 3

Which of the following statements, if either, is/are true in relation to dangerous dogs under the Dangerous Dogs Act 1991?

1. Where an offence has been committed under s. 1 of the Act, an authorised person working for a local authority has the same powers as a police officer to seize a dog.
2. The court may order the destruction of a dangerous dog, but only when an aggravated offence has been committed under s. 3(1) of the Act.

[A] Statement 1 only.
[B] Statement 2 only.
[C] Both statements.
[D] Neither statement.

Question 4

CRAWLEY was present at CADDICK's farm where a dog fight was taking place. He found out about it when he overheard the licensee of his local pub, GOUGH, talking about it to another customer. CADDICK was not present at the time of the fight, but knew it had taken place.

Who would commit an offence in these circumstances under the Protection of Animals Act 1911?

[A] CRAWLEY, CADDICK and GOUGH.
[B] CADDICK and GOUGH only.
[C] CRAWLEY only.
[D] CRAWLEY and CADDICK only.

Question 5

PRINCE owns a warehouse that has suffered a number of burglaries recently. He has employed WILKINSON as a security guard during the night when the warehouse is closed. WILKINSON takes an Alsatian guard dog to work and warning signs have been placed at all entrances to the premises. Every hour, WILKINSON walks around the yard surrounding the building, leaving the dog to roam around the inside of the premises while he does so. PRINCE knows that WILKINSON does this.

Have any offences been committed in these circumstances under the Guard Dogs Act 1975?

[A] Yes, an offence has been committed by PRINCE and WILKINSON.
[B] Yes, an offence has been committed by WILKINSON only.
[C] Yes, an offence has been committed by PRINCE only.
[D] No, as the dog has not been allowed to go freely on land.

Question 6

HARDING is a farmer and allows his sheep to graze on common land near his farm. KENT allowed her daughter LUCY, aged 17, to take her dog out on the common land, which was near their house. LUCY let the dog off the lead and it ran away from her and chased some of HARDING's sheep. LUCY eventually managed to control the dog before it attacked the sheep and none were injured.

Have any offences been committed under the Dogs (Protection of Livestock) Act 1953?

[A] Yes, by LUCY and KENT, but KENT would have a defence.
[B] No, because of the location of the sheep.
[C] Yes, by LUCY only.
[D] No, because none of the sheep were injured.

Question 7

The Animal Health Act 1981 creates certain powers for a constable, who has reasonable cause to suspect an offence has been committed, in order to control outbreaks of diseases amongst animals.

In relation to these powers, which of the following statements is correct?

[A] A power of arrest is provided for people found in the act of committing an offence only.
[B] There are no powers of arrest for a constable; offences may only proceed by way of summons.
[C] Offences committed under this Act have been declared arrestable offences under the Police and Criminal Evidence Act 1984.
[D] A constable may arrest a person in the act of committing an offence or where an offence has been committed.

Question 8

CARTER took his Jack Russell terrier into the woods one day to try to catch some badgers. He found a sett and sealed the exits, so that nothing could escape, and then put his dog inside. The dog came across a male badger, and a fight took place, resulting in severe injuries to both animals.

In these circumstances has CARTER committed an offence under the Protection of Animals Act 1911?

[A] Yes, in relation to the badger and the dog.
[B] No, this is not cruelty under this Act.
[C] Yes, in relation to the badger only.
[D] Yes, in relation to the dog only.

Question 9

Which of the following statements, if either, is/are correct, in relation to police powers under the Wild Mammals (Protection) Act 1996, when the officer has reasonable grounds for suspecting an offence has been committed?

1. There is no power to arrest a person who has committed an offence under this Act.
2. A constable may search a person or their vehicle using powers under this Act.

[A] Statement 1 only.
[B] Statement 2 only.
[C] Both statements.
[D] Neither statement.

Question 10

PARSONS was found one evening in the woods near his house by Constable BOWEN, who had received a report that a person was digging up a badger sett. When he arrived, Constable BOWEN found PARSONS digging earth on the surface area, but he had not disturbed the tunnels or the sett itself at this point. It turned out that the sett was no longer in use and no badgers were injured or disturbed, although PARSONS admitted he thought there were badgers present.

Which of the following statements would be correct in relation to the Protection of Badgers Act 1992?

[A] PARSONS commits no offence as no badgers were injured.
[B] PARSONS commits an offence of digging for badgers.
[C] PARSONS commits an offence of interfering with a badger sett.
[D] PARSONS commits no offence as no badgers were disturbed.

ANSWERS

Question 1

Answer **C** — Offences under s. 3 of the Dangerous Dogs Act 1991 may take place either in a public place (s. 3(1)), or in a place which is not a public place, but where the dog is not permitted to be (s. 3(3)). Answer A is incorrect for this reason.

There is a statutory defence under s. 3(2) of the Act, but this only applies where the owner of the dog passes control of it to a 'fit and proper person'. Therefore only Curson would be entitled to use the defence (but not in these circumstances). Even more importantly, the defence will only apply to offences committed under s. 3(1), i.e. in a public place. Answer B is therefore incorrect.

If the owner of the dog is under 16, the 'head of the household' would share liability with the owner. As Curson is *over* 16, this proviso does not apply and answer D is incorrect.

Question 2

Answer **B** — Section 1 of the Dangerous Dogs Act 1991 provides that no person shall allow the dog of which he is the owner (to which this section applies — including pit bull terriers) to be in a public place without a muzzle *and* a lead. The requirement to have both of these makes answer C incorrect.

A dog locked in a car which is parked in a public place is itself in a 'public place' (*Bates* v *DPP* (1993) 157 JP 1004), which makes answer A incorrect.

If a dog to which this section applies is kept muzzled *and* on a lead, and is in the charge of a person over 16, no offence is committed. However, since the dog was not on a lead, answer D is incorrect.

Question 3

Answer **A** — Under s. 5(1) of the Dangerous Dogs Act 1991 an authorised person working for a local authority *does have* the same powers as a police officer to seize a dog, where an offence under s. 1 of the Act has been committed. This makes statement 1 correct.

Under s. 4(1) of the Act, the court may order the destruction of a dog, where an offence has been committed under s. 3(1) (aggravated offence) *or* where an offence has been committed under s. 1 (dogs of a certain type which are controlled) and therefore statement 2 is incorrect.

Consequently, answers B, C and D are incorrect.

Question 4

Answer **D** — Only Crawley and Caddick commit offences in these circumstances.

A person who is present without reasonable excuse when animals are placed together for the purpose of their fighting commits an offence under s. 5A of the Protection of Animals Act 1911. Therefore anyone present at the fight would commit this offence.

Offences are also committed, under s. 5B of the Act, where a person publishes an advertisement for a fight between animals. The mere fact that Gough was talking about the fight, and was overheard, would not satisfy the requirements of this section, as he has not *published an advertisement*. Therefore answers A and B would be incorrect.

It is also a summary offence under s. 1(1)(c) to cause, procure or assist at the fighting of any animal, *or* to keep premises for that purpose. There is no mention of the person who 'keeps' the premises being present when the fight takes place and therefore Caddick would be guilty even though he was not there. (Answer C is incorrect for this reason.)

Question 5

Answer **A** — Under the Guard Dogs Act 1975, a guard dog must either be under the control of the handler at all times, or be securely fastened so that it is not at liberty to go freely about the premises. Clearly, when the handler is outside the building, he cannot be said to be in control of the dog, and if anyone were to break in, they would not be protected from the dog in these circumstances and therefore answer D is incorrect.

An offence is committed under s. 1 of the Act either by a person who *permits* the use of a guard dog on premises in contravention of the

Act (s. 1(1)), or by the guard dog handler (s. 1(2)). Answers B and C are incorrect for this reason.

'Premises' are land (other than agricultural land and land around a dwelling-house) *and buildings*, including parts of buildings, other than dwelling-houses (s. 7). Therefore the 1975 Act does not apply to dogs being used to protect houses or agricultural land (which includes fields, pig and poultry farms, allotments, nurseries and orchards).

Question 6

Answer **B** — An offence is committed under s. 1 of the Dogs (Protection of Livestock) Act 1953, if a dog worries livestock on any *agricultural land*. As the sheep were on common land, this offence is not made out.

If the incident had taken place on agricultural land, the owner of the dog, and if it is in the charge of a person other than its owner, that person also, would have committed an offence and answer C is therefore incorrect. (Note that answer A would have been correct in those circumstances.)

Answer D would be incorrect in any circumstances, as 'worrying' will include chasing livestock in such a way as may reasonably be expected to cause injury or suffering to the livestock.

Question 7

Answer **D** — This is not an 'arrestable offence' under s. 24 of the Police and Criminal Evidence Act 1984, but is a statutory power of arrest and therefore answer C is incorrect. Section 61 of the Animal Health Act 1981 states:

A constable may arrest without warrant any person whom he, with reasonable cause, suspects to be in the act of committing or to have committed an offence to which this section applies.

Answer B is therefore incorrect.

It extends beyond merely 'found committing' and therefore answer A is incorrect. There is also a power of entry provided, if necessary by force.

Question 8

Answer **D** — There are a number of ways in which a person may commit cruelty under s. 1(1)(a) of the Protection of Animals Act 1911 and one of these is to 'ill treat' an animal. This expression is quite broad, and in the case of *Bandeira and Brannigan* v *RSPCA* (2000) 164 JP 307, the defendant was convicted in the circumstances as set out in the question (making answer B incorrect).

An 'animal' for the purposes of this offence means any *domestic or captive animal*, which will include most forms of farm animal and domestic pets but not invertebrates (s. 15). An animal that has been temporarily captured will not necessarily be a captive animal for the purposes of the Act. Therefore, even though CARTER could be said to have been cruel to the badger, it would not amount to a specific offence under this Act. (Obviously, offences will have been committed under the Protection of Badgers Act 1992.) Answers A and C are incorrect for this reason.

Question 9

Answer **C** — Both statements are correct. There is no power of arrest under the Wild Mammals (Protection) Act 1996 but a police officer may search a person or their vehicle, when he or she has reasonable grounds for suspecting an offence has been committed under the Act.

Consequently, answers A, B and D are incorrect.

Question 10

Answer **B** — Offences under s. 1 of the Protection of Badgers Act 1992 relate to the actual killing, injuring, taking or attempting to do so of a badger.

Further offences can be committed under ss. 2 and 3 of the Act, of cruelty to badgers, digging for badgers or interfering with badger setts. However, in the case of *DPP* v *Green* [2001] 1 WLR 505, the Divisional Court held that the definition of a badger sett does not include the surface area above the system of tunnels and chambers. Therefore, if people are caught digging within this area, the charge ought to be the one under s. 2 (digging for badgers), and not s. 3A (interfering with a sett). (Answer C is incorrect for this reason.)

Section 1(2) of the Act creates a statutory presumption that a defendant was trying to kill, injure or take a badger if there is evidence from which that fact might reasonably be concluded. It is immaterial, therefore, that no badgers were disturbed or injured, or even that the sett was no longer active. Parsons has committed an offence simply by digging for badgers. (Answers A and D are incorrect for this reason.)

10 PREMISES

STUDY PREPARATION

The Criminal Justice and Public Order Act 1994 created several offences which have the effect of allowing the criminal courts to deal with offences of trespass. This chapter deals with offences such as trespassing with intent to disrupt lawful activities, trespassing with intent to reside on land, raves and residing in vehicles on land all of which are very topical.

Each offence has several elements to it, but there are common themes throughout, such as authorising officers, offences of failing to leave land when directed to do so and returning within three months of a direction being given.

The Criminal Law Act 1977 makes up the bulk of the second part of the chapter. Offences under ss. 6 and 7 of the Act are rarely used, but remain useful pieces of legislation, especially that of using violence for securing entry to premises.

Lastly, do not ignore the offences of being found on enclosed premises and causing a nuisance on educational premises; both are useful offences to remember.

QUESTIONS

Question 1

A supermarket is to be built on the outskirts of a town. Vehicles belonging to the building company have been parked in a compound on land owned by the supermarket, adjacent to the building site. The night after building had started, STIG, an eco protester, entered the compound and let down the tyres of all the vehicles, in order to disrupt work the next day.

Has STIG committed an offence under the Criminal Justice and Public Order Act 1994?

[A]   No, as he was not on land where the activity was due to take place.
[B]   Yes, he has committed an offence in these circumstances.
[C]   Yes, but only if it can be shown that work was disrupted.
[D]   No, people were not engaged in any activity when he acted.

Question 2

MARK intended to frighten his neighbour KAREN on Halloween night. He wore a mask and climbed into her garden, which was enclosed on three sides by hedges. He approached the kitchen window, where KAREN was standing and pressed his face against the glass. KAREN screamed and her boyfriend, HANK heard the noise and ran into the kitchen. He saw MARK in the garden and chased him. He finally caught him two streets away.

Does HANK have a power to deal with MARK for the offence of being found on enclosed premises?

[A]   No, the power to detain a person applies only to police officers.
[B]   No, as MARK was not on the premises for an unlawful purpose.
[C]   Yes, he may detain MARK in these circumstances.
[D]   No, because MARK was not found on enclosed premises.

Question 3

PARSONS, a farmer, agreed to allow a family of travellers to stay on his land for a week. Between them, the travellers had two caravans and three cars. After two weeks, they were still on the land and PARSONS asked them to leave. When they refused, he contacted the police.

Would the officers have the power to direct the family to leave the land?

[A] No, because the family did not have more than 12 vehicles between them.
[B] Yes, they could direct the family to leave the land, with their vehicles.
[C] No, because the family were originally given permission to stay by the landowner.
[D] No, because the family have not caused damage or used threatening/insulting behaviour.

Question 4

TOM and CAROL live together, but TOM has been violent towards her after drinking heavily. One evening, when TOM was in a pub, CAROL double locked the front door of their house to stop him getting in. When he got home, TOM lost his temper and began kicking the door to get in. CAROL was scared and called the police.

Would TOM be guilty of an offence under the Criminal Law Act 1977?

[A] No, because CAROL is not a trespasser on the property.
[B] Yes, but would have a defence as a displaced residential occupier.
[C] Yes, but would have a defence as a protected intending occupier.
[D] Yes, if it can be shown that he was aware CAROL was on the premises.

Question 5

EASTWOOD, is a caretaker at a school maintained by a local authority. He received a call from teachers that some youths from a different school were on the playing fields shouting and swearing at them. EASTWOOD telephoned the police and made his way to the field. He arrived before the police, to find several youths sitting next to a classroom quietly.

Which statement will be correct in relation to the youths causing a nuisance on educational premises?

[A] They may be removed from the premises by either EASTWOOD or the police.
[B] EASTWOOD has no powers to deal with the youths; he must wait for the police to arrive.
[C] EASTWOOD has no powers to deal with the youths, as the disturbance has ceased.
[D] EASTWOOD has a power to detain the youths until the police arrive at the school.

Question 6

Which of the following statements, if either, is/are correct in relation to an offence under s. 7 of the Criminal Law Act 1977 (person failing to leave premises)?

1. It is for the prosecution to prove that the premises were being used mainly for residential purposes.
2. A police officer must be in uniform to affect an arrest under this section.

[A] Statement 1 only.
[B] Statement 2 only.
[C] Both statements.
[D] Neither statement.

Question 7

Section 63 of the Criminal Justice and Public Order Act 1994 sets out the requirements for a gathering to qualify as a rave. Which of the following is true?

[A]   It would not be a rave if on common land, even in the open air.
[B]   A rave may take place on land partly in the open air.
[C]   It would not be a rave if on private land, even in the open air.
[D]   A rave must take place on land totally in the open air.

Question 8

Constable RAMIREZ received information that a rave was due to take place one evening. He attended the area to confirm the information.

Which of the following circumstances would provide a reason for a direction to be given for people to leave the land?

[A]   At least ten people were waiting for the rave to take place.
[B]   At least one person was preparing for the rave to take place.
[C]   At least two people were waiting for the rave to take place.
[D]   At least eleven people were waiting for the rave to take place.

ANSWERS

Question 1

Answer **B** — The offence will be committed when a person trespasses on land in the open air to intimidate people or obstruct or disrupt lawful activity (s. 68 of the Criminal Justice and Public Disorder Act 1994).

The lawful activity may be something which people are engaged in *or about to engage in* and therefore answer D is incorrect.

The offence is committed when a person trespasses on land where the activity took place *or on* land adjoining in the open air (which makes answer A incorrect).

There is only a requirement to prove that a person intended his or her actions to bring about the effects listed above. There is no need to show a successful outcome and therefore answer C is incorrect.

Question 2

Answer **C** — A person commits an offence if they are found in several places, including an enclosed yard, garden or area, *for an unlawful purpose.*

The case of *Smith v Chief Superintendent of Woking Police Station* (1983) 76 Cr App R 234 dealt with the issue of 'unlawful purpose'. The defendant was convicted after being found in the garden of a house peering through a window trying to frighten the woman inside. This makes answer B incorrect.

Answer D is incorrect because the person was 'found', by the boy-friend, and the premises were 'enclosed', by the hedges surrounding the garden. There is nothing in the Act which makes it necessary to have a walled enclosure.

Section 6 of the Vagrancy Act 1824 provides a power for any person to apprehend another person found committing the offence and take them to a justice of the peace, or more practically a constable. Answer A is incorrect. When a person has been 'found' on the premises, he or she can be arrested elsewhere (*R v Lumsden* [1951] 2 KB 513).

Question 3

Answer **C** — To prove the offence under s. 61 of the Criminal Justice and Public Order Act 1994, you need to show that at least two people are trespassing with a common purpose of residing there *and* reasonable steps have been taken to ask them to leave.

If the above conditions are apparent, you must then show that:

- they have damaged land, *or*
- they have used threatening etc. behaviour, *or*
- they have between them *six* or more vehicles.

As none of these apply, answers B and D are incorrect. Under s. 61(2), if the people had been given permission to stay on the land but had subsequently become trespassers, the officers would have to satisfy themselves that one of the conditions in s. 61(1) had occurred *after* they had become trespassers.

The original 1994 Act specified 12 vehicles, but this has been amended to six and therefore answer A is incorrect.

Question 4

Answer **D** — A person is guilty of an offence if they use or threaten violence for the purpose of securing entry to premises provided there is someone on the premises who is opposed to the entry *and* the person using/threatening the violence knows that is the case (s. 6(1) of the Criminal Law Act 1977).

The person would have a defence if they could show that they were either a displaced residential occupier (DRO) or a protected intended occupier (PIO).

To be a DRO, a person would have to show that they were occupying premises immediately before being excluded by a person *who entered those premises as a trespasser*. As Carol is not a trespasser, Tom would not be a DRO and would have no defence. Answer B is therefore incorrect.

To be a PIO, a person must have a freehold/leasehold interest in a property with two years to run. They must intend to use the property for their own occupation as a residence *and*, as above, they must have been excluded by a person who has entered the premises as a trespasser. As Carol is not a trespasser answer C is incorrect.

The fact that Carol is not a trespasser is the reason for Tom having no defence, which is why answer A is incorrect.

Question 5

Answer **A** — Where a person has caused a nuisance, disturbance or annoyance on educational premises, a police constable, or person authorised by the local authority, may remove that person from the premises (s. 40(3) of the Local Government (Miscellaneous Provisions) Act 1982 and s. 47(3) of the Education Act 1996). The power is to remove; not to detain, which is why answers B and D are incorrect.

Answer C is incorrect because the power to remove a person may be used even when the disturbance has ended.

Question 6

Answer **B** — Under s. 7(3)(a) of the Criminal Law Act 1977, it shall be a defence for the *accused* to prove that the premises formed part of premises used mainly for residential purposes.

The power of arrest applies to a constable in uniform only. As only statement 2 is correct, answers A, C and D are incorrect.

Question 7

Answer **B** — Section 63 of the Criminal Justice and Public Order Act 1984 applies to a gathering on land in the open air of 100 or more people, *whether or not they are trespassers*. Therefore a rave may take place on private land (making answer C incorrect).

Section 63(10) states that 'land in the open air' includes a place partly open to the air (therefore answer D is incorrect).

There is no reason why a rave may not take place on common land, which is why answer A is incorrect.

Question 8

Answer **A** — Under s. 63(2) of the Criminal Justice and Public Order Act 1994, a superintendent may give a direction for people to leave land if he or she reasonably believes that *two* or more people are making preparations for a rave to take place (therefore answer B is incorrect) *or ten* or more people are waiting for a rave to take place *or* ten or more people are attending a rave (therefore answers C and D are incorrect).

11 LICENSED PREMISES

STUDY PREPARATION

Once again, definitions are important; *do not* skip them at the beginning of the chapter in the Manual. Knowledge of the different types of licences is crucial, together with what premises they relate to.

Permitted hours are somewhat easier these days with all-day drinking, but watch out for extensions and permissions that can change regular hours. Ages are equally important, with the introduction of children's certificates and confiscation of alcohol adding to the equation.

Somewhat hidden at the end of the chapter are betting and gaming. These are also important areas to concentrate on. Even though the content has been scaled down in recent years, there is still a lot to get through; in particular the difference between the two definitions, and where betting and gaming can (and cannot) take place.

Lastly, you must be aware of powers to enter premises and, once inside, how to deal with *all* offences and behaviour/drunkenness.

QUESTIONS

Question 1

GREEN has opened a new restaurant. The opening night was so busy that he ended up asking some people to sit at the bar inside the restaurant to consume their meals, because of the lack of tables. While the group were eating their meals at the bar, they and other customers were being served intoxicants from the same bar.

In relation to the term 'bar', how have GREEN's actions affected the status of the premises?

[A] No change, as the group were consuming table meals, even though they were not seated at tables.

[B] No change, as the group were consuming intoxicants, which were ancillary to their meals.

[C] The status of the premises has changed to become a 'bar', as only those seated at tables may be served intoxicants.

[D] The status of the premises has changed to become a 'bar', as the group were not consuming table meals.

Question 2

Which of the following, if either, would be true, in relation to the definition of intoxicating liquor for the purposes of the Licensing Act 1964?

1. Any liquor with a strength not exceeding 0.75 per cent alcohol at the time of the sale is not included.
2. Shandy mixed by bar staff at the time of sale will be excluded from the definition, provided its overall strength is below that of proprietary shandy sold by retailers.

[A] Statement 1 only.
[B] Statement 2 only.
[C] Both statements.
[D] Neither statement.

Question 3

CARTWRIGHT was involved in a serious fight one night in The Royal Oak public house; he was arrested and charged. CARTWRIGHT was held in custody until the next available court, when the prosecutor produced evidence that CARTWRIGHT had threatened bar staff at two other public houses nearby on the same evening. The prosecutor applied for a two-year exclusion order against CARTWRIGHT for all three public houses.

Which of the following statements will be correct in relation to the magistrates' powers to grant the request?

[A] An order may be granted for all three premises for up to two years.
[B] An order may be granted for the Royal Oak only, for up to two years.
[C] An order may be granted for all three premises, for up to 12 months.
[D] An order may be granted for the Royal Oak only, for up to 12 months.

Question 4

Section 60 of the Licensing Act 1964 provides legislation in relation to permitted hours for premises covered by on-licences.

Which of the following would be permitted hours at such a premises on Christmas Day?

[A] 12.00 noon to 10.30 pm, with a break for four hours at a time to be decided by the licensee.
[B] 12.00 noon to 10.30 pm, with a break for four hours, beginning at 3.30 pm.
[C] 12.00 noon to 10.30 pm, with a break for four hours, beginning at 3.00 pm.
[D] 12.00 noon to 10.30 pm, with a break for three hours, beginning at 3.00 pm.

Question 5

West Hill Primary School is holding a quiz night to raise funds for new computers for the children. The head teacher, ANDREWS, has asked Constable THOMAS for advice on whether he can apply for an occasional permission to serve intoxicating liquor at the premises, and what restrictions there are on any profits made.

What advice should Constable THOMAS give ANDREWS in these circumstances?

[A] An application may be made, but the school may only make profits to recover their costs.
[B] An application may be made, and there are no restrictions on use of profits made.
[C] An application may not be made, as ANDREWS is not an on-licence holder.
[D] An application may not be made, as the school intend to make a profit.

Question 6

WALSH is the licensee of the Old Arcade public house and he is also on the committee of the local cricket club, which is organising a charity tournament. WALSH has been granted an occasional licence to serve intoxicants in a beer tent on the local playing fields, for the whole weekend, between the hours of 1.00 pm and 7.00 pm on both Saturday and Sunday. Constable BOOTH asks you what offences would be committed if intoxicating liquor was sold after 7 pm on both nights.

In relation to this question, which of the following statements is correct?

[A] On Saturday, WALSH would commit an offence of selling intoxicating liquor without a justices' licence.
[B] On Saturday, WALSH would commit no offence.
[C] On Saturday, WALSH would commit an offence of selling intoxicating liquor outside permitted hours.
[D] On either day, WALSH would commit an offence of selling intoxicating liquor without a justices' licence.

Question 7

In relation to an occasional licence, which, if either, of the following statements is/are correct?

1. A licence holder, who allowed a child under the age of 14 to be on premises, which are subject to such a licence, would commit an offence.
2. A licence holder would commit an offence if intoxicants were sold to a person under 18 at premises licensed under such a licence.

[A]   Statement 1 only.
[B]   Statement 2 only.
[C]   Both statements.
[D]   Neither statement.

Question 8

BERYL, the licensee of the Railway Inn, was working one Saturday evening at 11.15 pm, when she allowed two customers to leave the premises carrying their drinks in pint glasses. The customers were regulars, and she trusted them to return the glasses the next evening.

Have any offences been committed in these circumstances?

[A]   Yes, but only if the drinks were purchased after 11.00 pm.
[B]   No, because the intoxicants were taken away from the premises before 11.20 pm.
[C]   Yes, but only if the drinks were purchased before 11.00 pm.
[D]   Yes, regardless of when the drinks were purchased, or when they were taken away.

Question 9

STOREY, the licensee of the Flying Fox public house, was in his living quarters one evening. His deputy, HORGAN, was working in the bar, when he was observed serving a group of young people who were under 18 years of age by Constable HUSSEIN, who was in plain clothes. The group of people were allowed to consume their drinks in the bar.

What must the prosecution show in relation to STOREY's state of mind, in order to prosecute him for the offences of sale of intoxicants and consumption relating to someone less than 18 years of age?

[A] Guilty knowledge in relation to the sale of intoxicants, but not in relation to allowing them to be consumed in the bar.
[B] The prosecution does not need to show guilty knowledge in relation to either offence.
[C] Guilty knowledge in relation to allowing the intoxicants to be consumed in the bar, but not in relation to their sale.
[D] That STOREY either had knowledge of both offences, or that he turned a blind eye.

Question 10

In the Horse and Jockey public house, GILES, aged 18, went to the bar and ordered a pint of beer for himself, and another for his friend HARRISON, whom he knew was aged 17. PARRY, who was serving at the time, did not believe that HARRISON was 18 and refused to sell GILES the drink.

In relation to offences under the Licensing Act 1964, who of the above, if any, have committed offences?

[A] No offences have been committed, as GILES was not served with the drink.
[B] Only GILES of attempting to buy the intoxicants for consumption by his friend.
[C] No offences have been committed, as GILES is over 18.
[D] GILES, for attempting to buy intoxicants, and HARRISON for procuring GILES to purchase the drink.

Question 11

GRAY was in the bar of the Ship and Bottle public house on a Sunday afternoon with his son DAVID, aged 17. GRAY bought a pint of lager for himself, and another for DAVID. They took their drinks outside to the beer garden, where they drank them. GRAY is a personal friend of the licensee, HORTON, who was aware of DAVID's age.

In relation to the Licensing Act 1964, do any of these people commit offences?

[A] GRAY, for purchasing intoxicants for DAVID to consume, and HORTON for allowing a person under 18 to consume intoxicants.

[B] GRAY, for purchasing intoxicants for DAVID to consume, and DAVID for consuming them on licensed premises.

[C] No offences are committed in these circumstances.

[D] All three people commit offences in these circumstances.

Question 12

Constable SINGH was walking through a park, when he came across two young people, who were intoxicated. He discovered they were 15 years old and that they had been given drink by HAWKINS. Constable SINGH intercepted HAWKINS, who was walking away from the park and saw that he was in possession of four cans of lager. HAWKINS stated he was on his way home and intended to give the cans to his father. HAWKINS is over 18 years of age.

What are Constable SINGH's powers to deal with HAWKINS in these circumstances?

[A] He has the power to confiscate the intoxicating liquor from HAWKINS and demand his name and address.

[B] He has no powers, as HAWKINS did not intend to supply the intoxicating liquor to a person under 18.

[C] He has the power to confiscate the intoxicating liquor from HAWKINS, and report him for supplying intoxicating liquor to a person under 18.

[D] He has no powers, as HAWKINS is not in the company of a person under 18, to whom he intends to supply the intoxicating liquor.

Question 13

Which of the following places would be a 'relevant place', for the purposes of the Confiscation of Alcohol (Young People) Act 1997?

1. An off-licence.
2. A cinema.
3. A school playing field during the summer holiday.

[A] Place 3 only.
[B] Places 1 and 2 only.
[C] All of the above.
[D] Places 2 and 3 only.

Question 14

Constable KHAN was on duty as part of a plain-clothes team one evening. The team were tasked with visiting all the public houses in the centre of a town, to identify any under-age drinking. He arrived at the Royal Oak public house at 11.25 pm and identified himself to GEORGE, who was working on the door and asked to enter the premises. Constable KHAN was refused entry by GEORGE, who stated that the premises were about to close.

Does Constable KHAN have power to enter the licensed premises in these circumstances?

[A] No, the power to enter is restricted to uniformed officers only.
[B] No, the power to enter after permitted hours is restricted to a reasonable suspicion of an offence being committed.
[C] Yes, there is power to enter the premises to prevent or detect offences.
[D] No, the power to enter is restricted to 20 minutes after permitted hours have ended.

Question 15

JENNINGS has recently taken over as licensee of the Bluebell public house. The premises are frequented by a small group of locals, who enjoy a game of cribbage in their lunch hours. These people have queried with JENNINGS whether they can continue with their games, which involve a certain amount of betting.

In order to comply with the Gaming Act 1968, can JENNINGS allow them to continue?

[A]   Yes, there are no restrictions on gaming in a public house.
[B]   No, gaming on premises covered by a justices' on-licence is illegal.
[C]   No, the only gaming allowed on premises covered by a justices' on-licence is dominoes.
[D]   Yes, provided the game does not involve high stakes.

Question 16

WILKINS is manager of a betting office and one day BELL entered the premises in a drunken condition. Seeing his condition, WILKINS asked him to leave. BELL became abusive and started shouting. Constable GREEN was walking past as the incident occurred and heard the disturbance.

In relation to the Betting, Gaming and Lotteries Act 1963 only, what powers does Constable GREEN have in these circumstances?

[A]   Authority to enter the premises, in order to assist WILKINS to expel BELL under the Act.
[B]   Authority to enter the premises, but only if the constable suspected offences were being committed against the Act.
[C]   Authority to enter the premises, in order to expel BELL under the Act.
[D]   Authority to enter the premises, in order to arrest BELL under the Act.

ANSWERS

Question 1

Answer **D** — Section 201(1) of the Licensing Act 1964 defines a bar as including any place exclusively or mainly used for the sale and consumption of intoxicating liquor.

Certain places, such as restaurants in the main, become excluded from this definition (by s. 171) when they are set apart for the service of table meals which are accompanied by intoxicating liquor, with the following provisos:

- the sale of such liquor is confined to people *having those table meals and*;
- those parts of the premises are usually set aside for the service of table meals;
- the intoxicating liquor is ancillary to the meals being served, i.e. the food and not the drink, is the primary purpose of that particular part of the premises (this *does not* mean that drink can only be served to people who are seated at a table);
- a table meal will be a meal eaten by someone seated at a table (or at a counter or other structure which serves the purpose of a table), *which is not used for the service of refreshments for consumption by other people.*

A bit complicated, but the premises remain a restaurant while table meals are being consumed at tables, or counters, with drinks being ancillary to meals. However, this is only the case *as long as* the counter where the meal is consumed is not being used for the service of refreshments to other customers. Therefore when customers are no longer consuming table meals, the premises, status changes to that of a bar and answers A, B and C are therefore incorrect.

Question 2

Answer **D** — Neither statement is true. Any liquor with a strength not exceeding 0.5 per cent alcohol at the time of the sale is not included in the definition.

Shandy mixed by bar staff at the time of sale will *not* be excluded from the definition, even if its overall strength is below that of proprietary shandy sold by retailers. The sale of such a drink is treated as two separate sales of two different components. Shandy sold in cans or bottles will be below the prescribed strength, and are therefore not included in the definition (*Hall* v *Hyder* [1966] 1 All ER 661).

As neither statement is true, answers A, B and C are therefore incorrect.

Question 3

Answer **A** — Under the Licensed Premises (Exclusion of Certain Persons) Act 1980, the courts may exclude people from licensed premises. The power to grant an exclusion order applies to offences where violence has been used *or* threatened. An order may be granted for either one or more premises, depending on the circumstances and answers B and D are therefore incorrect. An order may remain in force for a period of between three months and two years and answer C is therefore incorrect.

Question 4

Answer **C** — Christmas Day hours are: noon to 3.00 pm with a mandatory 4 hour break, then 7.00 pm to 10.30 pm. This makes C the only possible correct option and therefore answers A, B and D are incorrect.

Question 5

Answer **B** — First, you need to recognise the difference between 'occasional permission' and 'occasional licence'. An occasional permission may be granted to a non-licence holder, whereas an occasional licence may only be granted to a licence-holder.

The Licensing (Occasional Permissions) Act 1983 allows licensing justices to grant 'occasional permissions' — that is, temporary authorities for the sale of intoxicating liquor — to organisations not operating for profit or private gain and therefore answer C is incorrect. If the profits from sales of intoxicants under the authority go to the club or organisation, this is not classed as private gain and therefore answer A is incorrect.

Although the school intends to make a profit from the sale, this is considered different from making a private profit or gain, as making a profit or gain is not the primary function of a school and therefore answer D is incorrect.

Question 6

Answer **B** — An occasional licence is issued to the holder of an on-licence for the sale of intoxicants at a place other than his usual premises. An occasional licence will set out the hours during which sales are permitted and may run for up to three weeks.

Normally, the two main offences relating to the sale of intoxicants in these circumstances are: selling intoxicating liquor without a justices' licence (contrary to s. 160 of the Licensing Act 1964) and selling intoxicants outside permitted hours (contrary to s. 59 of the Licensing Act 1964).

However, if an occasional licence is granted and intoxicants are then sold outside the specified hours *but* during the period when the occasional licence is still valid, there is no offence of selling intoxicating liquor without a justices' licence (*Southall* v *Haime* [1979] Crim LR 249), answer A is therefore incorrect. Walsh *would* commit an offence of selling without a licence *after* the occasional licence expired, if he sold it on the Sunday but since he would not commit the offence on both days, answer D is incorrect.

You would have expected Walsh to have committed the alternative of selling intoxicants after permitted hours on the Saturday. However, s. 59(3) of the Act states that the provisions preventing the sale of intoxicants outside permitted hours *will not* apply to intoxicants sold under an occasional licence and therefore answer C is incorrect.

There are options available for the police to make objections to any future licence applications if conditions are breached.

Question 7

Answer **B** — Section 168 of the Licensing Act 1964 prohibits anyone under 14 years from being in bars of 'licensed premises' during permitted hours. Because there are no 'permitted hours' for occasional licences, it would seem that there is no restriction in respect of children under 14 on premises, which are the subject of such a licence.

The offence of selling intoxicating liquor to a person under 18 years and the drinking of intoxicating liquor by such a person can be committed at premises licensed under an occasional licence. As statement 2 only is correct, answers A, C and D are therefore incorrect.

Question 8

Answer **D** — Section 59 of the Licensing Act 1964 states that intoxicants may only be purchased, consumed or taken away from licensed premises during permitted hours (in our scenario 11.00 pm).

Several exceptions are provided by s. 63 of the Act, one of which is the 20 minutes 'drinking-up' time. During this time, customers may drink intoxicants purchased before the end of permitted hours. They may also take intoxicating liquor away from the premises, provided it was purchased before the end of permitted hours *and* it is not contained in an open vessel. As the drinks are contained in open vessels, answers A, B and C are incorrect.

Question 9

Answer **D** — The holder of a licence or their servant may commit offences under s. 169 of the Licensing Act 1964 in the following circumstances:

- *Either person* — selling intoxicating liquor to a person under 18.
- *Either person* — knowingly allowing a person under 18 to consume intoxicating liquor in a bar.
- *The licence holder* — knowingly allowing any person to sell intoxicating liquor to a person under 18.

To prove the second two offences against the licensee, you must show knowledge on the part of the licensee and therefore answers A and B are incorrect. However, knowledge can include turning a blind eye (see *Buxton* v *Chief Constable of Northumbria* (1983) 148 JP 9) and therefore answer C is incorrect.

Such proof is *not* needed in respect of offences of selling to a person under 18. However, in the given set of circumstances, the licensee himself was not the person who sold the intoxicants.

Question 10

Answer **B** — Offences are committed under s. 169 of the Licensing Act 1964, if a person is under 18 and buys or attempts to buy intoxicating liquor or consumes intoxicating liquor in a bar (s. 169(2)) and therefore answers A and C are incorrect. A further offence is committed under s. 169(3), where a person buys *or* attempts to buy intoxicants for a person who is under 18, for consumption in a bar.

It is not relevant how old the person purchasing or attempting to purchase the drink is. No mention is made of procuring a purchase under the Licensing Act 1964 (although there may be a situation where a person is guilty of aiding and abetting) and answer D is therefore incorrect.

Question 11

Answer **C** — An offence is committed under s. 169(1) of the Licensing Act 1964, when in licensed premises the holder of the licence or his servant sells intoxicating liquor to a person under 18 or knowingly allows a person under 18 to consume intoxicating liquor *in a bar*. Under s. 169(3), a further offence is committed whereby a person buys or attempts to buy intoxicants for a person who is under 18, for consumption *in a bar*. As the drinks were not consumed in a bar, however, answers A, B and D are incorrect.

The operating part of this question is where the consumption was to take place. If the intoxicants were purchased for consumption in a bar by the person under 18, offences would have been committed by all three people. Obviously, if the police found out that this was regular practice in licensed premises, objections should be made to the licence being granted.

Question 12

Answer **A** — Under s. 1(1) of the Confiscation of Alcohol (Young Persons) Act 1977, a constable who reasonably suspects that a person who is in a relevant place (public place, etc.), is in possession of intoxicating liquor may confiscate the intoxicating liquor *and* demand a person's name and address if:

- the person is under 18 themself;
- the person intends that any of the liquor shall be consumed by a person under 18 in a relevant place;
- the person is with *or* has recently been with a person under 18 and that person has recently consumed intoxicating liquor in the relevant place. As this applies, answers B, C and D are therefore incorrect.

No offence is committed until a person fails to give their name and address or hand over the intoxicating liquor. Such a failure would provide the officer with a power of arrest.

Question 13

Answer **D** — A 'relevant place' under s. 1(6) of the Confiscation of Alcohol (Young Persons) Act 1997 would include:

- any public place, *other* than licensed premises (which includes an off-licence (option 1 is incorrect));
- any place other than a public place, to which the person has unlawfully gained access.

The first would include a place to which the public has access on payment. The second would not apply where a person gained access lawfully and later became a trespasser. (However, a person would presumably be a trespasser on school premises during the summer holiday.)

As option 1 is incorrect, answers A, B and C are also incorrect.

Question 14

Answer **C** — Under s. 186(1) of the Licensing Act 1964 a constable (not restricted to uniform) may enter (and therefore answer A is incorrect):

- Licensed premises and canteens — for the purpose of preventing or detecting offences against the Act — at any time during permitted hours and *30* minutes after the end of those hours (answers B and D are therefore incorrect). (For premises covered by an occasional licence — any time during the hours of the licence).
- Any licensed premises — at any time outside permitted hours where the constable reasonably suspects that an offence contrary to the Act is being committed, or is about to be committed.

Question 15

Answer **D** — Gaming is defined as the playing of a game of chance for winnings in money or money's worth (s. 52(1) of the Gaming Act 1968). There are restrictions placed by the Gaming Act 1968 as to where gaming can take place. It is a summary offence to take part in gaming in the street or in a public place (s. 5). However, gaming on licensed premises is permitted in certain circumstances and therefore answers A and B are incorrect. Customers may play cribbage, dominoes and other games (and answer C is therefore incorrect), approved by the licensing justices *provided* the games do not involve high stakes or the games are not used as an inducement to people to frequent the premises. In the given scenario, the games are played by local customers for low stakes; therefore such gaming would be permissible.

Question 16

Answer **A** — Under s. 10(2) of the Betting, Gaming and Lotteries Act 1963, the licensee may refuse to admit or may expel any person who is drunk, violent or quarrelsome. Under s. 10(3) of the Act, a constable may, on request of the licensee, *help* to expel such a person. Force may be used as necessary. There is a further power under s. 10(4) to enter premises to detect offences, but this is in addition to the power under s. 10(3). There are no powers of arrest for offences committed under the Act. As the power amounts to helping the licensee only, answers B, C and D are therefore incorrect.

12   DISCRIMINATION AND EQUALITY

STUDY PREPARATION

Although it would be easy to dismiss this area as merely a bit of political correctness, this chapter contains some of the most relevant and important legislation for supervisors and managers.

It is essential that all public servants understand their legal obligations in relation to the equal and/or fair treatment of others. In order to do so you need to know what will amount to discrimination, how to distinguish between direct and indirect discrimination and which groups of people are protected therefrom. It is also as important to understand the concept of victimisation and to recognise when and where it can arise.

When dealing with this area it is worth remembering that, in some circumstances, you have to treat everyone in the same way, while in others treating everyone in the same way is discriminatory — and if you don't understand this point you need to revise this chapter!

QUESTIONS

Question 1

Constable HUGHES has been asked out on a date by her Sergeant on several occasions. She always declines. Her Sergeant also makes several inappropriate and unwelcome comments to her of a sexist nature. Since Constable HUGHES has refused her Sergeant's advances she always has to perform foot patrol, and gets asked by the Sergeant to deal with all the menial tasks.

Is this victimisation as defined by s. 3 of the Sex Discrimination Act 1975?

[A] Yes, simply because HUGHES is being treated less favourably by the Sergeant.
[B] Possibly, but only if the Sergeant suspects that HUGHES intends to make a complaint about the treatment.
[C] Possibly, but only if the Sergeant knows for a fact that HUGHES has made a complaint about the treatment.
[D] No, as HUGHES is expected to perform any lawful duty when instructed by her Sergeant.

Question 2

The officer in charge of the family support unit has a vacancy, and would like the replacement to be a female officer. The officer has noticed that children or female victims seem to respond more positively to female officers. The officer wishes to place the following invitation in the advertisement of the post: 'On this occasion only female officers can apply for this post'.

In relation to this invitation which of the following is true?

[A] This is a case of a genuine occupational qualification and is not unlawful.
[B] This is direct discrimination and is unlawful.
[C] This is indirect discrimination and is unlawful.
[D] This is positive action and is lawful.

Question 3

A force motorcycle section has advertised a vacancy. One of the criteria is that the police officer must be able to pick up a Honda Pan European motor cycle (a large, heavy machine) from being on its side, and put it on its stand.

Is this a lawful selection condition?

[A]   Yes, it is a legitimate expectation of the job and must be able to be performed by all successful applicants.
[B]   Yes, provided the condition is the same for all applicants.
[C]   No, any condition other than one related to performance of duties is unlawful.
[D]   No, this is not a fair condition and could disadvantage some groups.

Question 4

The Armed Response Unit has advertised a 'familiarisation day for female officers only'. This is with the intention of recruiting female officers for a forthcoming firearms course, as they are under-represented in the department and below the Home Office target for minority officers. The selection process will remain the same as usual, and is open to all staff. Constable BRYAN, a male officer, is keen to get on the Unit and claims that he is being discriminated against, and that being able to attend this day advantages female officers.

Is the officer the victim of discrimination in these circumstances?

[A]   Yes, female officers would be disproportionately advantaged by this day and this is positive discrimination.
[B]   Yes, male officers are disadvantaged by this day and this is direct discrimination.
[C]   No, police forces are allowed to use affirmative action to target minority groups to reach target numbers.
[D]   No, police forces are allowed to discriminate in limited circumstances and this is one such occasion.

Question 5

Constable HEAL failed to attend a call for assistance from a colleague, and as a result the other officer suffered injuries. The injured officer, Constable STANLEY, who is African-Caribbean, believes that Constable HEAL did not attend the incident because of Constable STANLEY's ethnic background. Constable STANLEY intends to pursue a legal remedy.

Who may be liable in any future claim for discrimination on grounds of race?

[A] The Chief Officer only.
[B] HEAL only.
[C] Both HEAL and the Chief Officer.
[D] Neither, as the officer has not been discriminated against.

ANSWERS

Question 1

Answer **B** — In proving victimisation, the person must show that they suffered less favourable treatment as a result of their involvement in some form of action applying the 'but for' test (see *Aziz v Trinity Street Taxis Ltd* [1988] ICR 534). This means that 'but for' the action taken by the victim they would not have been given less favourable treatment. That action that the officer takes relates to any of the three main Acts in this area of legislation (Race Relations Act 1976, Sex Discrimination Act 1975 and Disability Discrimination Act 1995), and covers:

- Bringing any proceedings under these Acts.
- Giving evidence in proceedings under these Acts.
- Any act with regard to a person under these Acts, e.g. providing advice.
- Making an allegation about a person who may have contravened any of these Acts.

If the discriminator knows or suspects that the person has done any of these actions, or intends to, then less favourable treatment of that person amounts to victimisation. As the Sergeant's actions appear to amount to sexual harassment (which is covered by Sex Discrimination Act 1975), it is possible Hughes could be being victimised. In the question outlined, there is no evidence that the Sergeant is treating her differently simply because she has taken one of the actions therefore answer A is incorrect. Answer D is incorrect in that, even where the officer was expected to perform certain tasks, if she was treated differently using the 'but for' test then it would be discrimination. So we are left with a possibility of victimisation, and that does not necessarily have to be based on the knowledge of the Sergeant. Suspicion that she might complain would meet the 'but for' test and could be victimisation and therefore answer C is also incorrect.

Question 2

Answer **B** — Answer D is incorrect because positive action amounts to an encouragement of particular groups to apply for certain posts, under certain strict conditions, and here the officer's actions go way beyond simple encouragement. Answer A is also incorrect as a genuine occupational qualification (GOC) is where there is a legitimate reason (such as grounds of decency) to state that only certain groups may apply. Here there are no such grounds. An attempt to recruit female officers into a specialist department by excluding male applicants has been held to be unlawful in *Jones* v *Chief Constable of Northamptonshire Police, The Times*, 1 November 1999. It is direct discrimination because it is treating one group of people less favourably than others based on their sex. Answer C is incorrect because indirect discrimination involves setting the same criteria for a job, but the criteria are such that a significant proportion of people from a protected group are less likely to be able to achieve the criteria because of their membership of that group (e.g. a height restriction, which would affect female and some minority ethnic groups).

Question 3

Answer **D** — There is nothing inherently unlawful about setting legitimate conditions for a job vacancy (e.g. must have two 'A' levels) and therefore answer C is incorrect as it is too broad. However, any criteria must not disadvantage a significant proportion of people from a protected group. Simply setting the same condition for all does not make it lawful (e.g. 'applicants must be able to climb stairs' is the same for all, but would disadvantage wheelchair users) and therefore answer B is incorrect. Given the size and weight of the machine in the question, it is likely that fewer women than men could comply with the condition and it is this that potentially makes the requirement discriminatory and unlawful. Even if only one female officer could not comply with a condition of employment (as in *London Underground Ltd* v *Edwards* (No. 2) [1998] IRLR 364), it could still be indirect discrimination. As far as answer A is concerned, is it a legitimate requirement of the job? Imposing this requirement on all applicants appears to be far too broad, wholly unreasonable and, in relation to the differences in relative strength of male and female applicants, appears to disproportionately disadvantage the latter and therefore answer A is incorrect.

Question 4

Answer **D** — Positive discrimination involves selecting people in preference of others based on their membership of a minority group. The circumstances of the question do not amount to positive action because the selection process is open to all staff and therefore answer A is incorrect. As positive discrimination is unlawful in this country, answer C is incorrect. Direct discrimination is treating one group of people less favourably than others based on their sex and here the male officer has the same opportunity to apply for the post, and there is nothing to suggest selection will be on anything other than merit (therefore answer B is incorrect). Did the term discriminate in answer D put you off? Positive action, which this is, is a form of discrimination, but is lawful. An employer may discriminate if within the preceding 12 months there are no people or only a small number of people from a particular racial group or of a particular sex doing that work (in this case on the Unit) in a spccific locality.

Question 5

Answer **C** — Under the Race Relations Act 1976 the actions (or in this case inaction) of a fellow officer can attract liability to that individual under a claim for discrimination in addition to any claim that the victim might have against the relevant chief officer (see *AM v WC* [1999] ICR 1218). Both the Chief Officer and Heal are potentially liable and therefore answers A and B are incorrect. Discrimination is treating one group of people less favourably than others based on their sex, racial origin or marital status. There appears to have been discrimination and answer D is therefore incorrect.

13 OFFENCES AND POWERS RELATING TO INFORMATION

STUDY PREPARATION

At last! the final chapter — and a pretty straightforward one at that.

The management — and mismanagement — of information is an area of increasing importance to the police generally and therefore to its supervisors, managers, trainers and examiners.

The key issues here are the statutory restrictions on who can access what type of information and for what purpose. Much accessing of information involves the use of computers and it is necessary therefore to understand the relevant aspects of the Computer Misuse Act 1990.

QUESTIONS

Question 1

Constable BROWN has been asked by his neighbour to check the Police National Computer (PNC), as the neighbour wants to know if his future son-in-law has a criminal record. Constable BROWN agrees and conducts a PNC check on the person, and notices he has a record for offences of violence. Fearing the consequences, the officer does not want to tell the neighbour the truth, so he tells the neighbour that there is no criminal record. Constable BROWN is an authorised PNC operator, but realises he is not authorised to carry out a private check on behalf of his neighbour.

When does Constable Brown first commit an offence contrary to s. 1 of the Computer Misuse Act 1990?

[A] When he agrees to carry out the check.
[B] When he carries out the PNC check on the computer.
[C] When he views the data on the screen.
[D] When he gives the neighbour false information.

Question 2

DAVIDSON is a computer programmer who has been asked by JELLIS to assist in a crime. JELLIS wants him access the computer records of a Ferrari dealership's new customer's accounts and add JELLIS's details as a *bone fide* customer. This will, he believes, enable him to test drive a Ferrari. He intends not to return the car but take it for a 'joy-ride' amounting to an offence under s. 12(1) of the Theft Act 1968 (taking a motor vehicle or other conveyance without authority, etc). DAVIDSON 'hacks' into the company's computer and makes the changes. However, in reality, JELLIS will not be able to carry out his plan as the company always send a representative on the test drive.

Has DAVIDSON committed an offence under s. 2 of the Computer Misuse Act 1990 (unauthorised access with intent to commit arrestable offence)?

[A] Yes, even though the commission of the offence intended was impossible.
[B] Yes, even though he was merely facilitating the crime.
[C] No, as the intention to commit the crime lay with JELLIS.
[D] No, as the offence intended is not covered by s. 2.

Question 3

In relation to unauthorised access to computer under s. 1 of the Computer Misuse Act 1990 (hacking), consider the following 'actions'. In a situation where the access by the person is not authorised and they have the required intent and required knowledge, at which point would an offence under this section first be committed?

[A] When the computer is switched on.
[B] When the 'log on screen' is filled out.
[C] When they are successfully logged onto the system.
[D] When the actual programme is accessed.

Question 4

DAWLISH is a Crown Prosecution Service employee and is the prosecutor in a case of 'hacking' (s. 1 of the Computer Misuse Act 1990). DAWLISH received the papers from the police on Monday. On Friday, DAWLISH decided that the evidence produced by the police amounted to sufficient evidence to warrant prosecutions.

Within what period may proceedings for an offence under s. 1 above be brought?

[A] Six months from the Monday.
[B] Six months from the Friday.
[C] Twelve months from the Monday.
[D] Twelve months from the Friday.

Question 5

TURLEY has made an unauthorised modification of a computer program. In order to prove an offence of unauthorised modification of computer material contrary to s. 3 of the Computer Misuse Act 1990 it is necessary to show that the person had the 'requisite knowledge'.

What is that 'requisite knowledge'?

[A] That the modification will affect the operation of the program.
[B] That the modification will affect the operation of the computer.
[C] That the modification will prevent access to the program.
[D] That the modification was unauthorised.

Question 6

The Data Protection Act 1998 sets out data protection principles and schedules, which must be complied with. In relation to a particular police force, and its responsibility under principle 4 'personal data shall be accurate, and where necessary, kept up to date', which of the following people have direct responsibility for this principle according to s. 4 of the Act?

[A] The Chief Officer.
[B] The Data Protection Officer.
[C] The Data Controller.
[D] The person who puts the data on the computer.

ANSWERS

Question 1

Answer **B** — A person commits an offence under s. 1 of the Computer Misuse Act 1990 when they 'cause a computer to perform any function with intent to secure access to any program or data held in any computer'. This involves more than an agreement and therefore answer A is incorrect and more than simply looking at material on a screen and therefore answer C is incorrect. It does relate to an act completed on a computer and not on supplying personal information from such, whether true or false and therefore answer D is incorrect (although this may be an offence under other legislation governing data). In addition, the access to the data needs to be unauthorised, and the defendant knows it is unauthorised, which it clearly is.

Question 2

Answer **D** — Section 2 of the Computer Misuse Act 1990 requires intent on the part of the defendant, and this is either intention to commit an offence to which s. 2 applies, or the intention to facilitate the commission of such an offence. Davidson has this intention, as he knows the purpose of his actions and is aware that it will facilitate the taking and driving away (TADA) and therefore answer C is incorrect. Section 2 applies to the particular classes of offences set out under s. 24 of the Police and Criminal Evidence Act 1984, but this does not include those offences made 'arrestable' by virtue only of their inclusion in s. 24(2) of the 1984 Act. Section 12(1) of the Theft Act 1968 (taking a motor vehicle or other conveyance without authority, etc.) is such an offence and therefore answer B is incorrect. As to impossibility, s. 2(4) of the 1990 Act makes clear that a person may be guilty of an offence even though the facts are such that the commission of the further offence is impossible, but as the offence intended is not covered by s. 2 of the 1990 Act this is immaterial, therefore answer A is incorrect.

Question 3

Answer **A** — An offence under s. 1 of the Computer Misuse Act 1990 is committed by causing a computer to perform a function, and all the above answers would amount to 'functions'. As you were asked at which point would an offence first be committed, answer A is the correct answer. Although answers B, C and D all may fall under the section, they are incorrect as switching the computer on is the first function that would amount to the offence.

Question 4

Answer **A** — The period in which proceedings must be brought is six months and therefore answers C and D are incorrect. Time begins to run once evidence comes to the knowledge of the prosecutor and not when the prosecutor comes to the opinion that the evidence is sufficient to warrant proceedings (*Morgans* v *DPP* [1999] 1 WLR 968). This amounts to the Monday and therefore answer B is also incorrect.

Question 5

Answer **D** — To prove an offence under s. 3 of the Computer Misuse Act 1990 you have to show that the person had the requisite intent and the requisite knowledge. The knowledge is defined in the section, as the 'knowledge that any modification [the defendant] intends to cause is unauthorised'. This makes answer D the correct answer. The other three answers refer to the intent or *mens rea* the person has to have, which is defined in s. 3(2) as:

> . . . the requisite intent is an intent to cause a modification of the contents of any computer and by so doing—
> (a)   to impair the operation of any computer;
> (b)   to prevent or hinder access to any program or data held in any computer; or
> (c)   to impair the operation of any such program or the reliability of any such data.

Answers A, B and C are incorrect therefore as they refer to the requisite intent and not the requisite knowledge.

Question 6

Answer **C** — A crucial element in the Data Protection Act 1998 is the data protection principles set out in sch. 1. As well as introducing the principles, s. 4 of the Act makes it clear that principle 4 is the duty of the relevant 'Data Controller'. Answer C is the only correct option and therefore answers A, B and D are all incorrect.

Question 4

Answer **A** — The period in which proceedings must be brought is six months and therefore answers C and D are incorrect. Time begins to run once evidence comes to the knowledge of the prosecutor and not when the prosecutor comes to the opinion that the evidence is sufficient to warrant proceedings (*Morgans* v *DPP* [1999] 1 WLR 968). This amounts to the Monday and therefore answer B is also incorrect.

Question 5

Answer **D** — To prove an offence under s. 3 of the Computer Misuse Act 1990 you have to show that the person had the requisite intent and the requisite knowledge. The knowledge is defined in the section, as the 'knowledge that any modification [the defendant] intends to cause is unauthorised'. This makes answer D the correct answer. The other three answers refer to the intent or *mens rea* the person has to have, which is defined in s. 3(2) as:

> . . . the requisite intent is an intent to cause a modification of the contents of any computer and by so doing—
> (a)   to impair the operation of any computer;
> (b)   to prevent or hinder access to any program or data held in any computer; or
> (c)   to impair the operation of any such program or the reliability of any such data.

Answers A, B and C are incorrect therefore as they refer to the requisite intent and not the requisite knowledge.

Question 6

Answer **C** — A crucial element in the Data Protection Act 1998 is the data protection principles set out in sch. 1. As well as introducing the principles, s. 4 of the Act makes it clear that principle 4 is the duty of the relevant 'Data Controller'. Answer C is the only correct option and therefore answers A, B and D are all incorrect.